REFLECTIONS
OF AN
IRISH GRANDSON

A story of Grandmother Bridget (Meade) Quealy and the Meade family of Miltown Malbay, County Clare, Ireland

Vincent J. Quealy, Jr.
March 2023

THIRD EDITION

DEDICATION

I dedicate this writing—this history— to Joanie, my love of over 40 years. Joanie always listened with attention to all of my ideas and to my writing— draft after draft, revision after revision—adding thoughts, comments and suggestions all of which helped to make this long story a more understandable one.

And to my beloved children, daughters-in-law, son-in-law, and grandchildren, those glorious people who are such a joy in my life. Mo chroi mo thaisce. I very much wanted you to know your heritage, to understand the beauty and the sacrifice so bound together, to know the story of your family in Ireland that you might yet feel a stir when you look upon that lyrical place.

Hold it close, think of it sometimes and know from whence you came.

ISBN: 979-8-9876313-1-7
Printed in the U.S.A.
3rd Edition

INDEX

ACKNOWLEDGEMENTS

JIMMY MEADE
PAT MEADE
PETER MEADE
DR. JOHN TREACY
COLIN HENNESSY
PATRICK KIRBY
COLM HAYES
FRANK COSTELLO

I'm very grateful to all of those listed here for invaluable ideas, assistance, research suggestions, direct material and recollections, insights and commentary, all of which was both necessary and instrumental in the writing of this story. Each was generous with time and attention as I sought to assemble a clear story of events and "Troubles" which so deeply and tragically affected the townspeople of Miltown Malbay, and the Meade family particularly, in the period spanning the late 1880's through the Irish War of Independence.

The familiarity with the history of the time and the familiarity with the people who are principals in the story were essential to me in this project and it is those contributors listed here upon whom I relied for expertise.

Many thanks for your help and for your friendship.

PREFACE

IRELAND

"a terrible beauty is born"
– William Butler Yeats

Ireland suffered for centuries under British rule. It's well-known and well-recorded, a familiar truth to all. But I fear sometimes that the words are too easily written. The words are sometimes too easily spoken. We may nod in acknowledgement, though absent any full appreciation of the hardships endured or the miseries borne. The words are too broad, too general, too generic. The words merely declare that it is so, but carry no specifics, they describe no persons, no events, no effects of the cruel and terrible reign of the British Crown over it's Irish subjects.

But the effects were cruel and the effects were terrible and they stretched across centuries. It was in 1652, for example, that Cromwell completed his conquest of Ireland and it was then that Catholicism was banned and that all Catholic-owned land was taken and distributed among English-Protestant settlers. It was the beginning of a very long period of poverty and of anguish for Catholics unlucky enough to live in Ireland under the ruthless and oppressive rule of a colonial occupier. The taking of land from Ireland's Catholic population would have profound and tragic consequences for the next two centuries and more, perhaps never clearer than during the long torment of An Gorta Mor—the Great Hunger.

The horrors of the Famine descended upon the people of Ireland in 1845. Land ownership, at this time, remained almost entirely in the hands of Protestant landlords, many of whom were absentee landlords relying on Agents in Ireland to enforce collection of rents from their estate's tenant farmers. It's estimated that some 90% of land in Ireland was owned by such landlords at the time of the Famine, a direct result of Cromwell's ruinous confiscation of Catholic-owned properties 200 years earlier.

Tenant farmers were allowed only small tracts of land for use and were afforded no legal protections, but, rather, were merely tenants-at-will, subject to eviction at any time and for almost any reason. The small plots of land which they operated were often sufficient only to provide food for one family and to meet the regular rent payments due. The blight on the potato crop imperiled the ability of these farmers to succeed at either and the curse of evictions soon began. Throughout the period, tenant farmers then unable to satisfy rent payments owed to their Protestant landlords were mercilessly evicted and their cottages torn or burned down. Desperate families were now left both hungry and homeless.

Landowners, though, soon recognized opportunity for themselves amid the growing destitution of their tenants. Once families had been evicted and cottages destroyed, the newly-cleared land could be put into use for the more profitable practice of raising cattle and sheep.

While the British did not, of course, cause the Famine—the Great Hunger—neither did they offer any grand efforts to relieve it, beyond a few paltry and almost wholly ineffective measures. It was, in fact, a widely-held view among government leaders and influential economists in England that the Irish were themselves quite responsible for the famine calamity through a combination of over-populating the small farms on which they resided, poor and ill-suited farming practices and over-reliance on a single crop, the potato.

Worse, many believed, the very nature of the Irish character is defined by a lack of industry, of ambition, of enterprise. The Irish, in short, are simply "lazy". The notion of the Irish as "lazy" was plainly evident in some British expressions of the day. The planting beds spread across the small farms in Ireland, for example, were derisively referred to as "lazy beds".

Beset by starvation, disease and emigration, Ireland's population had, by 1851, been reduced by nearly three million people. All the while, thousands of Irish-bred cattle were continuously exported from Ireland to England in order to satisfy British appetites for beef.

The year 1857 saw the famine now past, yet new troubles arose and old troubles persisted. Conflicts over land reform, rack-rents, tenant farmer's rights, a continuing cycle of evictions and boycotts, anti-Catholic fervor and the ever-present tensions between the people and the Crown all remained firmly fixed in the daily life of the Irish.

Peter Meade, my great-grandfather, was born on January 1st of that year to John and Mary (Conway) Meade in Knockliscrane, Miltown Malbay,

County Clare. His story—the Meade family story— would now unfold amid the turmoil and the strife of the coming years.

And so it is well to remember and to appreciate the real history and not merely to rely on common and shallow refrains. It was, indeed, a long and difficult struggle before the Irish realized their destiny and "...a terrible beauty was born."

Vincent J. Quealy, Jr.
March 2023

MEADE FAMILY SUMMARY

NAME	DATE OF BIRTH	DATE OF ENTRY (US) - Age	RESIDENCE	DATE OF DEATH
Peter	01/01/1857		Miltown Malbay IRE	7/31/26
Ellen (Murtagh)	02/26/1857		Miltown Malbay IRE	11/20/43
Mary	05/14/1887	1906 - 19yrs old	Boston, MA	11/2/60
Bridget	10/3/1888	1909 - 20yrs old	Lowell, MA	12/28/86
John	05/01/1889	1908 - 19yrs old	Boston, MA	8/2/64
Patrick	03/15/1890		Miltown Malbay IRE	12/01/1890*
Margaret	05/04/1891	1912 - 21yrs old	Boston, MA	11/19/44
Anthony	02/04/1893	1913 - 20yrs old	Boston, MA	7/11/74
Thomas	05/04/1894	1913 - 19yrs old	Boston, MA	4/29/87
Patrick Jos	03/15/1896	1915 - 19yrs old	Boston, MA**	3/9/21
Joseph	04/02/1897		Miltown Malbay IRE	12/26/87
James	unknown		Miltown Malbay IRE	unknown***
Michael	09/09/1899		Miltown Malbay IRE	10/1/93
Catherine	8/24/01	1929 - 28yrs old	Boston, MA	3/13/91
Peter	2/1/03		Miltown Malbay IRE	5/12/21
James	4/19/05	1927 - 22yrs old	Boston, MA	3/23/84

* died of Bronchitis at age ten mos.
** after WW1, lived with Bridget in Lowell
*** died very soon after birth

CHAPTER ONE

"Deep-rooted Things"
Miltown Malbay, County Clare, Ireland

"My children may find here deep-rooted things."
W.B. Yeats

A British Member of Parliament, G. Shaw Lefevre, traveling throughout the West of Ireland in 1888, recorded that "From Ennis, I went to Miltown Malbay, a small town of 1,200 inhabitants, within a mile of the seacoast. It has been built under a system of 'leases for three lives', on land belonging to Mrs. Morony…the bay is an exceedingly pretty one, with a beautiful strand on hard sand; the Atlantic breaks upon the shore with its full power. With the pure air and the beautiful coast scenery, the place ought to have a future before it, now that there is direct communication by railway". How sadly mistaken was Lefevre's prediction of Miltown Malbay's future.

The town has only existed since about 1800 but grew rapidly: by 1821 it had a population of six hundred residents. During the Great Famine (1845 — 1852) many farmers were evicted by the unpopular Morony family, major landlords with extensive holdings throughout the area. In the years after the famine the Protestant Morony family continued with practices of rack-renting and evictions.

Eventually, the population arose in protest and organized a boycott. The British responded predictably and harshly, imprisoning all pub-owners and shopkeepers who refused to serve the family or their servants. By the end of 1888 most pub-owners and shopkeepers were in jail.

During the Irish War of Independence there were a number of incidents in Miltown Malbay. A large number of the town's residents gathered, on April 14, 1920, at the main intersection in the town—known as Canada Cross—celebrating the release of Irish political prisoners from Mountjoy Prison. It infamously resulted in the Shooting at Canada Cross when members of the Royal Irish Constabulary (RIC) and the Royal Highland Infantry Regiment fired into the crowd wounding seven and killing three: John O'Loughlan, Thomas O'Leary and Patrick Hennessy.

Miltown Malbay was also the site of the Rineen Ambush, which took place on the main road to Lahinch and Ennistymon. On 22 September 1920, a Royal Irish Constabulary lorry was ambushed there by the Mid Clare Brigade of the Irish Republican Army (IRA), in retaliation both for the killing of Martin Devitt, a key leader in the IRA, at Crowe's Bridge earlier in the year and for the massacre at Canada Cross. Six officers of the Royal Irish Constabulary were killed in the ambush.

Reprisals by the British followed quickly as the Black & Tans, a specialized British military unit, rioted in Ennistymon, Lahinch and Miltown Malbay, killing six people and burning twenty-six buildings, including the Town Halls at Ennistymon and Lahinch. I've outlined much more about each of these incidents in the story which unfolds in the following pages.

Miltown Malbay was served by the West Clare Railway for many years, operating from July of 1887 until February 1, 1961.

Willie Clancy, one of the greatest uilleann pipers in Irish musical history, was born and lived in the town. He left an important and enduring legacy to traditional Irish music. His life and work is commemorated and celebrated through the *Scoil Samhraidh Willie Clancy* which annually attracts musicians from all over the world to Miltown Malbay.

Once, while visiting with my cousin Pat Meade in Miltown Malbay, I learned that another Meade cousin, Joanie Madden, is a renowned Irish musician, with scores of albums produced and sold both as a solo artist (Irish whistle instrument and flute) and as a member of a very successful Irish musical group which she founded, "Cherish the Ladies". Joanie's mother, Helen (Meade) Madden, was born and raised in Miltown Malbay before emigrating to New York City. Helen Meade's father, Jim, and Bridget Meade, my grandmother, were first cousins.

Another of the parish's famous sons is Dr. Paddy Hillery, who was Ireland's first commissioner to the European Economic Community before serving two terms as President of the Republic of Ireland from December 1976 through 1990. Dr. Paddy Hillery's father, Dr. Michael Hillery, figures prominently in the history of Miltown Malbay during the period of the War of Independence and in the story of the Meade family at that time.

Surely, it is an Irish town which, from its founding, struggled to exist for many years through the Famine, through the Land League conflicts and boycotts, through evictions, through "The Troubles" and terrible reprisals taken by British soldiers and through the War of Independence. At the entrance to St. Joseph's Church, a landmark and center of life in the town, stands a granite monument reading:

In memory of those who in this parish did not receive a proper ritual burial, who died early in pregnancy, who died before or at birth, who died without Baptism, who were lost at sea or at war, who perished from the Armada, who were not properly buried during the Famine. Each of their lives had significance and here we honour and remember them. May they rest in peace.

The main street and square remain today (2022) much as it looked one hundred years ago in photos of the period. Some businesses of that time actually do still remain, such as Maguire's Forge on Ballard Road. Sarsfield Maguire was one of the "three brave blacksmiths" who, in 1881, were jailed for refusing to shoe the horses of the landlord Mrs. Ellen Burdett Morony after her eviction of tenants from her property.

The town is little noticed by tourists to County Clare, excepting the annual Willie Clancy music festival noted earlier. It is a town, rather, quite undisturbed by the pace of the world, still home to life-long residents, most known to one another and most of familiar surnames: Quealy, Meade, Curtin, Conway, Hennessy, Burke, Maguire, Kerin, Frawley, Hennessy, Malone et al.

I recently came to learn a bit about this long-standing intimacy among the townspeople of Miltown Malbay, evident even now. While planning my June 2022 meeting with Pat Meade in Miltown, I telephoned Peter Meade (Pat's brother in Westwood, MA), to ask about how best to reach Pat. Peter remarked that I only need to "...get to town and ask for Pat." Amused and charmed by the thought, I nevertheless requested Pat's telephone number.

Pat and Michael and Gerard Meade and cousin Joanie Madden live still today in Miltown Malbay and Jim Meade's granddaughter from Boston, Hillary Meahl, chose to be married very nearby, in Doolin, in July 2022.

I visited with Pat Meade in Miltown Malbay in June 2022 as we had, earlier that Spring, agreed to spend some time in discussing and supplementing my family research. We arranged to meet in the parking lot of the Super Valu Store, just a block behind the Main Street shops, on Tuesday, June 7th. He arrived precisely at the time we had discussed, 10:15am. We'd talked by telephone a couple of times before my arrival on this date in Miltown

Malbay and were prepared for a day spent together reviewing places and sites of importance to the Meade family story and especially to the story of three Meade brothers—his dad, Joe, and his uncles Peter and Jim—during the Irish War of Independence. Pat knew much about the family's history and about events during the time of the War of Independence.

He brought me to the site of the Rineen ambush; to Crowe's Bridge in Inagh; to see Maguire's Forge; to the mural depicting the famous "three brave blacksmiths"; to Ballard Cemetery; to the original Meade farm; to the intersection of Canada Cross; to Spanish Point, the center of Morony family power and influence in the area. All of these people and places and their significance to the story are described in the pages which follow.

Pat took a great interest in my research and in the detail which I'd compiled, adding many insights and observations as we drove throughout the Miltown Malbay area that day. He'd known principals in the story of the IRA's Mid Clare Brigade—Patrick Kerin, Anthony Malone, Martin Frawley and others— in their later years and spoke of them knowledgeably and with real admiration. He was very generous with his time, not hurried nor even aware, it seemed, of the many hours already spent together on that June day.

Sometime around 3:30pm, or maybe 4:00pm, I said to Pat that I was very appreciative of the time he'd afforded me and did not wish to impose any longer. Pat shook his head, dismissing the thought. "I've nothing to do and all day to do it" he told me. The humor is genuine and authentic to the Irish personality—to Pat Meade's personality—underlying a kind and generous nature, unwilling to hint at any inconvenience to himself and glad to accommodate my agenda.

I had, in fact, arrived in Miltown Malbay on the morning of my meeting with Pat Meade much earlier than necessary, planning to spend a bit of time making notes and crafting a few essential questions for the day while enjoying some coffee and perhaps a local bakery treat. I found myself, however, unable to locate a bakery or a coffee shop open before 10:00am.

Noticing an older gentleman walking toward me, I asked if he might direct me to a shop or café. "Oh" he replied "not in this town now, not before 10 O'Clock…it's a small town you know". "But" he continued "walk with me now while I get my paper just there and they'll have a take-away (take out)."

We walked along a short distance, the older gentleman telling me that he was born in this town "…in that blue house", pointing ahead. I introduced myself and told him that I was here this morning to meet with my cousin, Pat Meade. Astonished, he stopped walking, looking at me directly now with an air of excited discovery. "Well, I'm your cousin too, I'm Chrissy Curtin." Pat Meade's mother is Mary (Curtin) Meade. I remembered then Peter Meade's instruction to me of a few months earlier as he'd insisted that it's only necessary to "...get to town and ask for Pat." So it is in Miltown Malbay.

It is both remarkable and of some curious comfort to me that a Quealy or a Meade can travel from Boston to this little town on the West Coast of Ireland in the year 2022 and still encounter residents who are immediately able to identify you as a cousin. Deep-rooted things, indeed.

CHAPTER TWO

First Memories

I knew, from my very first childhood memories, that I was Irish and that I was surrounded by Irish relatives: my paternal grandparents, both of whom emigrated to the US in their early adulthood, aunts, uncles and an ever-present cousin, Eileen Meade. Eileen was a nun in the order of the Sisters of St. Joseph and a constant companion of my aunt Helen, known as Sister Ernestine, in that same order of nuns.

It was almost never my father who made any clear mention of Ireland, but my paternal grandmother, Bridget Meade, who made it most plain, as she still spoke in a very strong and a very unmistakable Irish accent. She was born to a tenant farmer in County Clare, Ireland, and lived her early life as most poor Irish Catholics did at the time: under harsh and repressive conditions of Protestant and Anglo-Irish (direct descendants of English Protestants) landlords and the rule of the Royal Irish Constabulary (RIC).

I have clear and sharp memories of my grandmother throughout my early childhood, as I would accompany my father on most Saturdays to visit her in her Brookline apartment. She held to many old Irish expressions of speech, often greeting me by declaring "well, isn't it Himself." The apartment was thick with Irish lace placed on various tables and I remember old and withering Palms, saved from Palm Sunday, stuck behind a Crucifix. I definitely had the impression that my grandmother was poor, as the apartment was quite dull and dark and she dressed in what appeared to be very old and very un-stylish long dresses and nylon stockings that were too short. She wore a net over her hair, which was short and fully gray.

The visits were generally brief— maybe an hour or so—but over time, I heard many stories of Ireland directly from my grandmother. Stories about a Banshee that haunted stormy nights in Ireland and about how dogs would surely know when someone was approaching death. She told me how dogs would grow silent and almost unresponsive, as if already grieving, in a signal that the death of a family member was near. My paternal grandparents kept an Irish Wolfhound in still another nod to an Ireland which I now know they both loved very deeply.

I remember a few Shillelaghs in the apartment and was told that they were very helpful as an aid in walking around the Irish countryside. I was given a Shillelagh as a gift on a couple of different occasions, though I don't remember exactly if those occasions were birthdays or Christmas or maybe First Communion. And I still sing an old Irish lullaby—"Tora Lora Lora"—to my grandchildren, that lilting and soothing lyric I first learned at the knee of Bridget Meade.

Visits with aunts, uncles and cousins were also routine and commonplace throughout this period of my childhood. I have particularly fond memories of time spent with my Uncle Tommy's children, my cousins Noreen, Sheila and Mary Quealy. The story of their place in our family is especially complicated and sad at the same time.

While I'm unclear on every detail, the general story is that Tommy was stationed for a time in England during World War II, prior to his service in Germany in Patton's Army. He had earlier attended Trinity College in Dublin, which adds greatly to support the fact that Ireland was very much a place of keen importance and meaning in the family, even if not to my father.

Tommy met and married a young Mary Josephine Hennessy during the time that he was stationed overseas. Mary Hennessy was born in Tipperary, Ireland on March 24, 1924. She was twenty years old and working in the Bromley section of London at the time of her wedding to Tommy and the two were the parents of my three cousins mentioned earlier, Noreen, Sheila and Mary.

It gets a bit foggy from there, but apparently some years after the war, Tommy met and became much involved with Catherine ("Rena") Di Terlizzi, eventually leaving Mary and the girls, marrying "Rena" and parenting two more daughters.

My family kept a regular and close relationship with Mary and my three cousins from Tommy's first marriage for at least several more years and I know that my uncles and aunts did as well. Some of the extended family may have maintained a relationship with Tommy and "Rena", but we certainly never did and I really only ever met Uncle Tommy once or twice and never with "Rena" and their two daughters—my unknown cousins.

The lilt of old Irish expressions was steady and normal whenever we gathered with family members, which was not infrequent in those years. One nephew or niece was said to "have the map of Ireland" on his or her face, another to have received the "gift of Blarney" and uncles—especially Larry—had a funny little ritual of placing their palms against our ears and lifting us only a few inches off the floor and asking "can you see Ireland"?

All of this was set, as I noted, in the early part of my childhood and visits to my grandmother's apartment ended quite abruptly by the time I was twelve or thirteen years old. Sadly, I never saw my grandmother after this age and was given only the cursory explanation that she was now resident in a nursing home, Marion Manor in South Boston, and that my father visited her regularly, so no need for any of us to do so.

The same was true for family gatherings with aunts, uncles and cousins. Sometime around early adolescence, we stopped visiting with them and I only saw any of them after this time on very rare occasions and never really knew anything about their lives except what a child might remember.

I was, of course, taken with all of the usual interests of a twelve or thirteen-year- old boy, focused on sports and Summer friends and a girlfriend or two and paid little attention to the gradual disappearance of these people and of these influences in my life. And yet, this Irishness stayed with me, lingered with me and dwelt in me always. It would awaken again in the years to come and would arouse in me a keen and irresistible desire to learn and to know everything about my Irish ancestry and about the lives of my grandparents and other relatives who lived in Ireland. It would ignite in me a true love for Ireland and it lives in me today.

Interestingly, it was the Meade side of the family—and not the Quealy side—that was in the forefront and dominant in any family stories and remembrances and it was the Meade side of the family that would host, from time to time, large family reunions. I remember one such large family reunion held at the George Wright Golf Club in Hyde Park and I remember that all of us in my immediate family attended. My father was not at all enthusiastic about attending and, rather, made clear to us all that the entire event was of little interest to him and that we would attend only owing to family obligation.

I was aware of my father's disdain for the reunion and even for the idea of celebrating an Irish ancestry which he seemed not to embrace and in which he had no apparent interest. I'm very unsure about why he did not speak of his own family's history in Ireland or why he never imparted to me any particular importance of it. It is all the more unusual when I now consider that the legacy surrounded him and that his own parents, grandparents, aunts and uncles—John and Bridget (Meade) Quealy, Peter and Ellen Meade, John Meade, Jim Meade, Joseph Meade, young Peter Meade, Katie Meade—held fast to it and were, in fact, devoted to Ireland throughout their lives. Many had been fully engaged in the Irish struggle for independence, including service in the Irish Republican Army (IRA). Peter Meade's death in 1921 at the age of eighteen came as a direct result of his activities while attached to an Active Service Unit (ASU) of the Mid Clare Brigade of the Irish Republican Army during the Irish War of Independence. Military Pension Archives record that "...conditions endured by him, while on the run from British forces, led to his illness and death."

Captain Edward Lynch of the 4th Battalion, Mid Clare Brigade, writing in support of a posthumous Military Pension for Peter Meade (Ellen Meade, his mother, as beneficiary) declared that "...his people have always been connected with the national movement." James Hennessy, Officer Commanding (O/C), 4th Battalion, Mid Clare Brigade added that "...she (Ellen Meade) always spent any spare cash that she had with those that were interned or on the run...". It was not, of course, unusual to be either interned or on the run in early twentieth century Ireland.

John Meade and Jim Meade remained dedicated to Ireland's cause even after arriving in the US, serving in leadership roles of multiple Irish organizations and associations including: The Eire Society, County Clare Association, Ireland's 32 (Jim Meade was president of the group and its name is a reference to the unification of Northern Ireland's 6 counties with the 26 Counties comprising the Republic of Ireland), the Clare Club, The Central Council of Irish County Clubs, the Friends of County Clare and the Irish Social Club of Boston.

The two uncles, together with Aunt Katie, lived in and immediately around Dorchester after leaving Ireland and for the entire remainder of their lives, always just a very few miles from their sister Bridget and nieces and nephews including, of course, my father. Certainly, he knew them and certainly he knew something about their lives and their interests, especially as they were prominent in Irish organizations and associations of the time, even receiving recognition in local Boston media. Not really ever, though, was I made aware of any of these relatives or of their stories. It saddens me, actually, to realize that two great-uncles and a great-aunt of mine, each with so much personal Irish and family history to hear about and to learn from, lived so nearby me for all of my life and yet they remained quite purposely hidden from view.

Instead, my father spoke of these Meade relatives—his grandparents, aunts, uncles and cousins—with a bit of indifference, with the single exception of his aunt Katie, Bridget's sister. Katie was only spoken of in reverent terms and with great admiration, as she had sacrificed so much of her personal life—even remaining unmarried—to care for her nieces (Catherine, Maura and Cathleen) and her nephew (Peter) whose mother, Mary (Shine) Meade (wife of Katie's brother, John) had died tragically, along with her fifth baby, Anna, during childbirth on February 7, 1930 in a Boston hospital. The sudden tragedy and loss of a wife and mother and newborn infant daughter left John's family in very difficult circumstances.

Katie had arrived in Boston from Ireland only a few months before, on October 9, 1929, uncertain about whether or how long to remain in the US, but, at her brother John's request, now undertook the role as caregiver to the family. Katie Meade was then twenty-eight years old. She put herself to the task and was a steadfast, committed, loving and ever-present "adoptive mother" to John Meade's four children until her death, at age 90, on March 31, 1991.

Ellen Meade wrote of her daughter Katie that "...I let her (Katie) go to America to try and help us pay it (bank debt)...her oldest brother, John, his wife and baby died in hospital leaving four young children, he went out to where she worked asking her to come with him to take care of his four children...she told me she could not refuse him he was so good to us all when they were young, which he was...".

Aunt Katie also, through the years, returned periodically to Miltown Malbay. Pat Meade, during my visit with him in June 2022 in Miltown Malbay, spoke about Katie with deep affection and recalled her unfailing humor and humility, even to moments before her death. Pat, living in Quincy, MA at this time, tells of the Sunday morning he was called to Milton Hospital by Dr. Cronin in order that he might visit briefly with Katie before she died in the coming hours. Pat's wife, Mary, had spent many years as a Nurse at Milton Hospital and was caring for Katie in her hospital room that day. Pat, as he tells it, entered Katie's hospital room and she immediately greeted him saying "...so nice that you came to visit Mary at work...".

Oddly, however, my father sometimes—though rarely— betrayed a sentimentality for Ireland in unguarded moments. At times, when he might feel reflective or feel the tug of a warm reminiscence, he would tell a story, as it must have been told to him, of his father, John Quealy, as a young boy in

Ireland. The story is thick with the superstitions of the old Irish, but was told and re-told by my father on different occasions through the years:

John was sent out one stormy and threatening night to find and retrieve the family's cow, a treasured and vital resource on any small farm in Ireland in the early 1900's. The wind howled and the rain pounded as John strode across familiar pastures at first, but as he walked on with no sight of the family cow, he grew disoriented and cold and tired. The light from a window of a nearby house drew his attention and he knocked on the door and found himself greeted by a kind old woman who quickly ushered him in out of the cold and the wind. He was warmed by the fire—a peat fire, no doubt— and the old woman comforted him with warm milk and biscuits. She bade him stay the night to regain his strength and return to his search in the clear of the morning.

John awoke early and, with the storm long past, set off to resume his search for his family's cow, which he found quite easily now in the still, calm of the morning. He reached home and explained to his worried family that he'd been sheltered from the dangers of the storm and the cold night by the kind old woman in the house just beyond the hill. Startled, his parents told him that no such house and no such old woman had ever been a neighbor near their farm and they all set off to locate the house and the woman. But no house and no kind old woman were ever found in the fields or hills nearby.

And once, riding in my car while I was playing songs from an Irish music playlist, the beautiful old Irish song titled "I'll take you home again, Kathleen" started playing over the speakers. My father stopped conversation in mid-sentence to say that the song had been his father's favorite and he immediately began to sing each verse, not missing a single lyric.

It's also true that my father often used old Irish expressions in his speech, remarking on the clever personality of one friend or another by suggesting that "...he didn't get it from the wind" or catch-phrases of Irish humor such as "it's not a fit night outdoors for ye...let your brother do it" or even a personal and unique family favorite of his own father's, used to describe anyone who's talent might somehow have impressed him: "he ought to be on tely-vision".

And, in an unusual nod to his ancestral homeland and, perhaps, his unspoken wish that I should know something about it, my father presented me with Leon Uris's wonderful book entitled *Ireland: A Terrible Beauty* as a gift on my twenty-fifth birthday. I wondered then—and I wonder still—about his choice of that particular gift and if it somehow represented his recognition that Ireland held importance in our lives, though he was himself reluctant—even unwilling—to say it. It is a curious thing.

John Quealy, my grandfather, emigrated from Ireland and arrived in Boston in June of 1910. Some years later, in completing his 1917 US Military Draft Card, John clearly indicated his own loyal support for an independent Ireland and his avowed Irish Republicanism when, required to list his "nation/state "of origin on the government form, he wrote: "none until Ireland gets national independence."

It is a remarkable and poignant declaration given that the Easter Rising of 1916 had taken place only several months earlier and John Quealy, by early 1917, was now boldly refusing to identify his homeland as a part of the United Kingdom, though it remained then securely so. It surely appears that Quealys—as well as Meades—held strong and deep affection for their native Ireland and for its national ambitions.

I have written here, in the story that follows, all that I know and all that I have learned of our Meade family from Miltown Malbay. It is a remarkable story of hardship and of persistence; of oppression and of defiance; of suffering and of courage; of cruelty and of rebellion and most especially it is a story of struggle to aid and to witness a beloved homeland—a beloved Ireland—find its rightful place among the free nations of the world, to wrest from the grip of a brutal oppressor this beautiful isle.

I have researched extensively and every date, fact, place and event is both accurate and corroborated, cross-referenced against different sources: the Military Archive Service Pensions Collection, files of the Mid Clare Brigade, the Clare Library, the Bureau of Military History, the Irish Family History Centre, The Epic Museum, irishgenealogy.ie, The Clare Heritage Centre, recollections of direct Meade family members accompanied by original writings, documents and memorabilia, conversations and/or correspondence with Professors Mike Cronin of Boston College, Frank Costello of Queens College, Belfast, Colm Hayes of the North Clare Historical Society, Dr. John Treacy, PhD, historian and researcher, member of the Clare County Council and author of "The Story of County Clare and its People", John Galvin, Managing Director of The Clare Champion newspaper, Colin Hennessy, Curator of the Mid Clare Brigade website and member of the Mid Clare Brigade Commemoration Committee, Patrick Kirby, Historian assigned to the Irish National Defense Forces, each of whom suggested rich and invaluable research material.

References to people and events that appear in the writings of Ellen Murtagh Meade, Jim Meade, John Meade, Dr. Hillery, Seamus (James) Hennessy, Ned Lynch, Ignatius O'Neill and of other prominent persons in Miltown Malbay at the time of the Irish War of Independence match with precision the history of the time and unveil a town and its people that felt the terrible wrath of Crown forces. And those writings unveil, as well, a family which felt the full weight of that wrath and yet endured.

Without a personal story, however, we can read only dates, times, places, a mere recounting of facts, unable to evoke pain, unable to evoke suffering, unable to evoke bravery, unable to evoke cruelty, unable to evoke fortitude and purpose. It is only the stories—the personal stories—of the people in those places, on those dates, at those times which make history talk to us and it is those personal stories which are my great advantage in this writing.

It is from people close by to events recalled here and in the following pages—from sons, grandsons, granddaughters, nieces, nephews—that I have uncovered insights which moved so many of our Meade family to boycott rents, to resist in full the occupation of their beautiful land, to leave a beloved home, to bid farewell to cherished family.

And the history is very real. Boycott they did, resist they did, sacrifice they did, cry farewell they did. We know, surely, that the broad and general story of Irish suffering has been told and re-told. The story of the Meade family, though, has been awaiting a time for the telling. I am glad and I am proud now to tell it.

The grand Irish poet, W.B Yeats, once wrote: "I am of Ireland....come dance with me in Ireland." And so, I will.

CHAPTER THREE

Peter, Ellen and the Farm

Peter Meade was born to John and Mary (Conway) Meade on January 1st, 1857. I know almost nothing about his very early life and begin to uncover information about him in the period of the early 1880's. Peter, by then some twenty-three or twenty-four years old, was a tenant farmers' son and now politically and morally opposed to the wealthy and favored landlords who had so long exercised authority and control over much of Ireland's land, farms and pastures.

The landlords of these properties were often cruel and unfeeling, having solidified that reputation during the famine, the Great Hunger, when they continued forced evictions of even the most destitute and desperate of tenants.

The Protestant Morony family in the West of County Clare were such landlords. Peter Meade would set himself against them and took up a leading role in the Miltown Malbay community promoting and supporting ideas and policies for land reform and for tenants' rights.

Advocating for land reform and organizing meetings of local tenant farmers in 1880's Ireland, still fully under harsh British rule, required great courage and posed many risks. Major political leaders of the land reform movement had been arrested and jailed by British authorities for such transgressions.

Peter, during this time-frame, became increasingly active as a proponent of land reform and was a leader among local supporters of Charles Stewart Parnell and the Irish National Land League, which Parnell had helped form in 1879 and of which he served as president.

The Land League, as it was more commonly known, had set two very clear and principal aims among its resolutions, which were:

1. "...to bring about the reduction of rack-rents
   (excessively high rents) and
2. "..to facilitate the obtaining of the ownership of the soil by
   the occupiers."

Parnell was arrested in Dublin on October 12, 1881 and held at Kilmainham Gaol after agitating against England's Second Land Act because it did not provide tenant farmers with relief for rent-arrears or rent adjustments made necessary by poor harvests. Two days later, the Land League was banned.

Leadership of the Land League eventually came to believe that mere political opposition and strategies would not suffice to move the British Government to adopt more favorable terms or policies for Irish tenant farmers. More assertive measures, it was clear, would be required. Parnell and other imprisoned Land League executives then adopted the idea of withholding rent payments from landlords and wrote the "No Rent Manifesto" from their prison cells on October 18, 1881. It called for tenant farmers of Ireland "... to pay no rents under any circumstances to their landlords..." and it was published on the front page of "United Ireland" on October 22, 1881.

Peter Meade, now inspired it appears, by the "No Rent Manifesto" and undaunted by the arrests of its authors, continued his efforts to organize tenant farmers in and around Miltown Malbay. Rent boycotts were planned and implemented across County Clare and throughout Ireland by respected leaders among the Country's legion of tenant farmers and, eventually, produced the intended effect. The British Government under Gladstone finally negotiated the Kilmainham Treaty, whereby the Government agreed to expand the Second Land Act to include provisions offering some relaxation of payment terms for tenant farmers in arrears.

It may have seemed to many that the broad, national boycott of rent payments had succeeded in its purpose with the adoption of the Kilmainham Treaty, but, locally in Miltown Malbay, the Morony family was unbowed.

The Morony's had operated as landlords in Miltown Malbay and in the surrounding area since the early 1800's and, just as they had exercised distinct cruelty during the Famine, persisted with the practices of rack-rents and evictions into the late 1880's.

A particular incident which occurred in 1881 galvanized local resistance against Mrs. Ellen Burdett Morony, a landlady with holdings in the Spanish Point area of Miltown Malbay. Mrs. Morony, early in that year, evicted a number of tenants from the farms which they were operating, thereby drawing the ire of most residents in the town. Shortly after the evictions, Mrs. Morony sent some of her horses into town, to village blacksmiths, to be shod. The blacksmiths, however, refused to do the work and were immediately imprisoned. The three blacksmiths were sentenced to 28 days in prison—one day for each nail that would have been used to properly shod her horses.

The families of the three blacksmiths—McGuire, Heaney and Moloney—were supported by villagers throughout the Miltown Malbay area during the term of imprisonment. The bravery of the three blacksmiths remains a powerful remembrance in the town still today. A large mural depicting the three at work in a forge adorns the entire side of a two-story building at the corner of Ballard Road and Main Street. Jim Meade wrote admiringly of the three brave blacksmiths in one of his poems:

On foreign coasts proud Miltown boasts, three blacksmiths, bold and brave
Though old and frail, they went to jail, their neighbours homes to save
No tarnished gold their hands would hold, no tyrant could them pay
Their graves God guard in bleak Ballard, near old Miltown Malbay

Struggles to advance the rights of tenant farmers and to achieve the right "... of the ownership of the soil by the occupiers" continued in Miltown Malbay, encouraged and nurtured by Peter Meade and by other well-respected leaders among the people of the town. Fr. Patrick White, parish priest of St. Joseph's Church in Miltown Malbay, was such a leader.

Fr. White invited Charles Stuart Parnell to visit Miltown Malbay and to address the area residents. Impressed by the work and the resolve of Fr. White and of the townspeople to stand full-strength for important reforms and to defy even the most powerful landlords, Parnell accepted. He addressed a crowd of some 20,000 people gathered in Miltown Malbay from across all parts of County Clare on January 26, 1885. Parnell told the crowd assembled that day that County Clare was at the very vanguard of support for the Land League, proving an example for all the rest of Ireland.

Peter Meade, at age twenty-eight, married Ellen Murtagh on February 15, 1885 at St. Joseph's Church in the center of town. Ellen was days shy of her twenty-eighth birthday and the youngest of John and Bridget (Bellet) Murtaghs' six children. Fr. Patrick White married the couple.

Only weeks after the wedding, in March of 1885, it was announced at

Buckingham Palace that His Royal Highness Prince Albert, the Prince of Wales, would visit Ireland in April. Fr. White, decrying the visit, wrote in a letter to the Nationalist party newspaper "United Ireland" that "I regard any display of welcome, in the present circumstances of our country, to an English Prince, as degrading to our national character." Such a public and written rebuff of a member of the British Royal Family, was, in 1885 Ireland, near treason.

Opposition to British rule in Ireland, though, was fervent in Miltown Malbay and expressed unafraid and with vigor by Fr. Patrick White, officiant at the wedding of Peter and Ellen Meade. Sure it was that enmity toward rule by a foreign monarch was shared between priest and parishioner.

Together, the newly-wed couple operated a small farm as tenants and raised a large family of fourteen children in the Townland of Knockliscrane, Miltown Malbay, County Clare. Perhaps in a portent of sorrows to come, the young parents' fourth child, Patrick, born on March 15, 1890, died of bronchitis at the age of ten months. It was customary in Ireland then for a child born in later years to take the name of a sibling who had died in infancy. Such was the case when Patrick Joseph Meade was born, precisely and oddly on the same day and month as his deceased brother Patrick, though six years hence: March 15, 1896. And, sadly, the name "Patrick" would confer upon its new namesake yet another ominous fate some years ahead.

Only a few years later, another son, James, died very shortly after his birth. Following custom and as with Patrick, the couple later gave the name "James" again to the fourteenth and last child born to them.

Land reform frictions had earlier prompted the first full-scale effort at valuing all properties owned or leased in all counties of Ireland. The project had gotten underway in 1830 and was led by Sir Richard John Griffith. Griffith had been appointed as Commissioner of Valuation in 1827 and charged with surveying and recording land boundaries in Ireland and with identifying both landowners and any tenants in occupancy. The work was tedious, time consuming and detailed and was not completed until 1865. His work was titled the "General Valuation of Rateable Property in Ireland". It was generally referred to, though, as the Griffith Valuation Books.

The Griffith Valuation Books of 1855 list John Murtagh (Ellen Murtagh's father) as leasing a "...house, office (shed) and land..." at Ballinoe, County Clare. The land was ten acres and three Roods and valued at 3 Pounds Sterling/10 Shillings. The house alone was valued at 10 Shillings, bringing a total valuation for all of the leased property to 4 Pounds Sterling—the approximate equivalent of $600 US dollars in 2022. The Clare Heritage Centre states that "...the above holding was, of course, the property that... Peter Meade 'married into'." The system of "Leases for Three Lives", which prevailed in Ireland at the time, allowed for a lessee to designate persons other than immediate family members to assume the lease, persons such as John Murtagh's son-in-law, Peter Meade. Considerations included the health and age of a new lessee, intending to maximize the length of the lease, as well as the benefit which might still accrue to a direct family member, in this case, Murtagh daughter, Ellen. Francis Gould Morony was the landlord of the farm on which new tenants, Peter and Ellen Meade, now resided.

Strained and difficult relations among landlords, tenant farmers and shop-owners continued for many more years. A determined group of town leaders and shopkeepers organized a boycott aimed directly and singularly at the Morony's and, over the course of several days in February 1888, refused to open their shops and pubs to any Morony family members, to any employees of the Morony's or to the police, the Royal Irish Constabulary. The Clare Journal reported on Monday, February 13, 1888 that "...all attempts of the police and military to procure food or refreshments were unavailing. In every case, the proprietor refused to open his establishment." Court Summonses were quickly issued to the leaders of the protest, charging "... conspiracy to compel...persons...from dealing with certain members of the Royal Irish Constabulary".

Prosecution of the protest organizers was completed in just four days, on February 17, 1888, and resulted in an agreement by eleven of the protesters to end their boycott and to guarantee the supply of goods to the Constabulary in the future. Eleven other defendants prosecuted that day refused such a guarantee and were sentenced to a month's imprisonment. The Clare Journal of that date records that "The prisoners were removed under a heavy military and police escort to Ennis last evening."

Peter Meade remained among the leaders of the tenant farmers and townspeople of Miltown Malbay in lending his voice to the cause of securing for tenant farmers the right to land ownership, steadfast, outspoken and courageous in his ambition for meaningful and substantive land reform. He encountered much hardship in his efforts, but not much success.

Writing a few years later of his devotion to fairness for Irish tenant farmers and of his determination to defeat the long and implacable history of landlordism, Ellen Meade wrote "...my dear husband fought hard during that time as he never missed a meeting and the opposition sent a priest into our house to try and change him, but he said he could not turn his back on him that had done so much for us all (a reference to Parnell)...he had troubles galore but his country was always his trouble and every one of his children are the same at home and away...".

The Meade family continued working the small ten-acre farm in Miltown Malbay and, taking on significant debt with a loan from The National Bank, it was purchased in 1916, "...just as the trouble was coming..." Ellen Meade later wrote. Peter Meade was, by then, fifty-nine years old.

Ownership of the farm on which Peter had raised his young family and on which he had worked for so many years earlier as a tenant farmer, represented, for him, the aspirations of a lifetime.

It represented, also, the gravest of disappointments on realizing that, despite long hard hours of work, every day in every season, he'd not likely ever be able to repay the mortgage held by the National Bank. Peter died very suddenly working on his farm in 1926 at sixty-nine years of age and just ten years after its purchase. Ellen wrote some time after his death that "...when he saw he could not pay anything it prayed so much on his heart that he died suddenly without saying one word to us...". His obituary records that "...he was a devout Catholic, patriotic Irishman...a keen follower of Parnell and was connected with all his movements, especially that one which was so beneficent to the people, the 'No Rent Manifesto'."

The National Bank, a short few years later, did re-possess the farm pending payment arrangements pledged by Joe Meade. "The Bank has the farm until the money is paid", wrote Ellen Meade, "and you know my worry at that, having to part our home after all that is suffered in it."

The Note was paid, the Bank satisfied and brothers Joe and Michael continued operating the farm in Miltown Malbay for many years.

Ellen (Murtagh) Meade died on November 20, 1943 at the age of eighty-six years old. She's buried at Ballard Cemetery with husband, Peter, and other Meade family members. The cemetery sits only a short distance from what had been the family's ten-acre farm and from the town center of Miltown Malbay.

CHAPTER FOUR

Bridget's Voyage

Bridget Meade, my paternal grandmother, was born in Miltown Malbay, County Clare, Ireland on October 3, 1888, one of fourteen children of Peter and Ellen Meade. She lived her childhood and adolescent years, even into her early adulthood, on the ten-acre farm which the family then occupied as tenant farmers.

Bridget and her brothers and sisters, though poor and bound to the long struggles endured by all Irish subjects of the Crown, did find happiness in the grand beauty of the landscape surrounding them and in the company of one another during their early childhood years. Jim, the youngest child in the family and a poet by avocation, wrote many years later that "...we young Meade's climbed lofty leeds at the edge of closing day; what joys were found in the hills around my own Miltown Malbay...".

Many millions of Irish had, sadly, found it necessary to leave their homes and their homeland as oppression, penal laws, famine, rack-rents, anti-Catholicism and more beset them for centuries. Bridget found herself now numbered among them by 1909, departing her home, her family, her native land and sailing on the SS Saxonia from Queenstown, Ireland, in that sorrowful year. The big ship left its berth on June 2, steering a true and steady course for America, but for many aboard—for Bridget Meade— steering, as well, toward an unclear and an uncertain future.

It is a measure of how entirely the British set about purging Ireland not only of its land and of its resources, but of its language and of its history and of its culture, that the very harbor from which Bridget Meade sailed in 1909 was known then as Queenstown. It had long been known, actually, as Cobh, its Irish name, and was a sleepy little fishing village at the southern edge of County Cork, near the River Lee. It was the potato famine—the Great Hunger—that changed the story of Cobh.

The potato blight and resulting famine struck in 1845 and between then and 1849 over 2.5 million desperate Irish emigrants found passage from Cobh Harbor on hundreds of sailing ships and steamers bound for America.

The conditions aboard often seemed hardly better than conditions in the Irish countryside and many died en route from rampant disease. The ships carrying Ireland's poorest sons and daughters soon became known as "coffin ships" and Cobh Harbor as the "Harbor of Tears".

And yet, in 1849, while Cobh Harbor was still the key port of departure for so many suffering Irish, the British cheerily renamed this port of Irish grief "Queenstown" in honor of Queen Victoria's visit there. A final irony, however, remains in that the HMS Titanic, the "unsinkable" pride of British shipbuilding and symbol of the Empires' maritime preeminence, left Queenstown—left Ireland's Cobh Harbor—as its last port of call before heading across the Atlantic for its maiden voyage on April 11, 1912.

Bridget Meade is listed on the passenger manifest of the SS Saxonia as having departed from Queenstown, though it is sure that she departed from the "Harbor of Tears."

A young Bridget Meade arrived—alone—in Boston on June 10, 1909, no doubt anxious and unsure about what awaited her in this distant and unfamiliar land. She was far from all that she had known, far from all that she had cherished and still quite unwelcome in this new place which had very little regard for poor and Catholic Irish immigrants. "The worst misfortune which ever happened to the United States" said Mr. Arthur Crew Inman of Boston's old Brahmin society "...is the Irish". Her life had changed utterly. She was then twenty years old.

Irish songwriter Brendan Graham, in his beautiful ballad "Isle of hope, Isle of tears", wrote movingly of a young Irish girl, Annie Moore, leaving home and arriving at Ellis Island on January 1,1892. It was the official Opening Day of the renowned immigration center and Annie Moore from Ireland was the very first immigrant to be processed at Ellis Island. She was seventeen years old. "Courage is the passport when your old world disappears..." reads a line from Grahams' song. Such was Bridget Meade's passport.

Bridget settled in Lowell, MA and found work there as a domestic, attending to household chores and duties for Sydney and Gertrude Bailey and their two young children, Edward (9) and Helen (2). Sydney Bailey was a Jeweler by trade and owned a number of shops in the Lowell area. The 1910 US Census lists the Bailey home at 73 Forthill Avenue, Ward 9, Lowell, MA. Bridget Meade is identified as "household member" and her "Relationship to Head of Household" described as "servant".

Many Irish immigrants throughout the 1840's were attracted to Lowell by the city's need for unskilled workers to fill jobs in textile mills and factories. Workers who were native and local to the area had begun, by this time, to agitate for higher wages, shorter working hours and safer conditions. Irish immigrants presented mill and factory owners with an ideal opportunity to simply ignore the demands of local workers and to thwart the growing threat of unions. The newly-arriving Irish were hired in large numbers, very willing to work long hours for low pay. A large community of Irish was established over the years in Lowell and it was not by coincidence that Bridget Meade found her way there. Bridget's Aunt, Catherine Meade, had emigrated to America in 1868 and, after arrival in Boston, soon settled in Lowell where she found work as a waitress in one of the city's hotels.

Interestingly, Bridget returned to Ireland in June of 1913 and stayed for better than four months' time, returning to Boston from Ireland in October, having once again departed from Cobh Harbor, this time aboard the SS Franconia. Bridget was accompanied, on this voyage, by her brothers Anthony and Thomas. It appears that Mr. Sydney Bailey may have agreed to this four-month interruption in Bridget's domestic service to the household, as, upon return to Boston and registering with US Customs, Bridget still listed her occupation as "servant", presumably in the employ of Mr. Bailey.

It's unclear how Bridget met John Quealy, also of County Clare, Ireland and born in Inagh, quite nearby Miltown Malbay. John had left Ireland and emigrated to the United States in June of 1910, a full year after Bridget, arriving in Boston aboard the SS Ivernia after a crossing originating in Cobh Harbor.

It is known, by a review of a US Military Draft Card dated January 6, 1917, that John was then employed as a Wool Sorter at the US Worsted Company in North Chelmsford, MA. He listed his residence on that Draft Card as Lowell, MA, apparently having made his way to the deep Irish community and to the plentiful employment opportunities for poor and unskilled immigrant workers found in that city in the early part of the twentieth century.

Perhaps it was here in this city of so many Irish immigrants that John Quealy and Bridget Meade first met, improbably if so. John Quealy's family home in Inagh, County Clare, measures only ten miles from Miltown Malbay and the Meade family's farm, yet it seems likely the two first met in Lowell, MA—more than 2800 miles from the West Coast of County Clare.

Bridget and John were married at St. Aidan's Church in Brookline on June 4, 1919. Both John and Bridget then listed their residence as Brookline. Bridget lists her occupation on the Brookline Record of Marriage as "maid" and John lists his as "janitor".

While living in Brookline during this period of 1919, Bridget was employed as a domestic maid by Mrs. Rice, according to family memories. A bit of research uncovers that a Mrs. Elizabeth G. Rice lived in a stately home on Wellington Terrace in Brookline and owned a boarding house on Cypress Street. She was the widow of a prominent local attorney, David Hall Rice.

Though I cannot be certain that it was this very Elizabeth Rice who employed Bridget Meade as a domestic maid, it is reasonable to believe so. Mrs. Elizabeth G. Rice, at the very least, matches Bridget's known employer by surname, by city, by time-frame, by means and by ownership of the boarding house. Further still, the 1880 US Census lists Elizabeth G. Rice, then age 35, and spouse "D.H." (little doubt, David Hall) Rice resident at East Merrimack Street, Lowell, MA. Elizabeth Rice surely would have been familiar with the sprawling Irish immigrant community in Lowell and able, in the years ahead, to find suitable staff there for the boarding house which she later owned in Brookline. Coincidences are narrowed to probabilities.

Soon, though, the newly-wed couple returned to Lowell where they started a young family and lived for at least the next several years. Five of John and Bridget's children—John, Thomas, Vincent, Helen and Lawrence—were born in Lowell between April 1920 and September 1928.

It was in Lowell, at 36 Webber Street, where a sorrowful chapter unfolded for Bridget and John Quealy. Patrick Joseph Meade, the fourth of Bridget's ten brothers, had emigrated to the United States in September of 1915 and first lived with their brother, John, in Boston. A short few years after his arrival in the United States, President Woodrow Wilson asked Congress, on April 6, 1917, to declare war on Germany after multiple US merchant ships were sunk by the German Navy. Congress obliged and Wilson's "War to End All Wars" was underway.

Patrick Joseph Meade soon was drafted and first assigned to the American Expeditionary Forces (AEF), 52nd Engineer Battalion, Company C. The 52nd Engineer Battalion was first constituted in August of 1917 and was deployed in France. Private Patrick Meade and troops of the 52nd Engineer Battalion departed Hoboken, NJ aboard the ship "Aeolus" on June 7, 1918, bound for a fate which none of them could know and which none of them could escape.

The Battalion encountered dangerous and major combat on the front line, having "...the difficult mission of constructing and repairing the railroads that were the logistics life of the AEF."

The 52nd Engineers suffered a German attack of Mustard Gas late in the Summer of 1918, near Verdun, during the Aisne-Marne Offensive and Pvt. Meade was grievously injured. The Great War would end only some three months later in November, 1918.

While it is likely that Patrick Meade was first treated for his exposure to Mustard Gas at a rudimentary field hospital, it is known that he remained in France for six months after the gas attack, not departing for his return to the United States until February 1919, a full three months after wars' end. It's clear from this time frame that Patrick Meade's injuries were sufficiently serious to prevent his transport home.

The field hospitals were ill-equipped, of course, for both the volume and the severity of injuries then occurring. A system of "hospital trains" for transporting seriously wounded soldiers was developed and the trains could move large numbers of critically-injured soldiers to Base Hospitals, which served as the key facilities for treatment and recovery.

The Base Hospitals were originally planned for a population of about 500 beds each, but that proved to be woefully and sadly too few. "...In crises, they were expanded to 2500 beds..." and many patients were eventually moved to convalescent camps to continue often long and difficult recoveries. According to the World War One Centennial Commission "...there were inevitably long-term patients...and those casualties had to have somewhere to recover...". The Convalescent Camps served that purpose.

I do not have specific information about Patrick being treated at any particular Base Hospital nor convalescent camp, but it seems sure that he was, judging from the time period which elapsed between his injury and his departure from France.

He boarded the ship "Mercy" at the port of Bordeaux, France, on February 27, 1919 and is listed among a number of war casualties traveling on that vessel and assigned to "Convalescent Detachment #146 Bordeaux." The "Mercy" arrived at New York on March 12, 1919 and by that year's end, Patrick Joseph Meade had moved to the house at 36 Webber Street, Lowell, and to the care of Bridget and John Quealy, convalescing there from injuries suffered during his military service and from a number of surgeries which were undertaken over the course of the next year. He was officially discharged from the US Military on June 27, 1919.

Tragically, Patrick Joseph Meade—the second Meade son given the name of Patrick—died from the effects of exposure to Mustard Gas on March 9, 1921, six days short of his twenty-fifth birthday. He's buried at St. Joseph's Cemetery in West Roxbury, later joined there by brother John and sisters Margaret and Catherine (Katie). It would not, for Bridget, be the last death of a brother at a very young age and it would not be the last death of a brother resulting from military service.

The 1930 US Census next finds the large—and still growing—Quealy family living in Brookline where the last two of seven children—Theresa and Brendan—were born between January 1930 and August 1933.

The address listed for the family on the US Census Form of 1930 is an apartment at 62 Cameron Street, #130, Brookline. It was just a few years later that the Quealy's settled into a home at 29 Summit Avenue in Brookline. The Quealy children would attend the nearby St. Mary of the Assumption School, founded in 1899. John Quealy was then employed by the Town of Brookline Highway Department, assigned to the Department's Cypress Street yard.

During my most recent visit with Pat Meade in June of 2022, he told wonderful stories about "Aunt Bridgie", recalling that "she stayed very much connected and in-touch with family news and with other events in Miltown Malbay". "Bridgie", he said, "was the best source and the most knowledgeable about things then (early 1900's)...she told about dances with friends and neighbors and making a bit of trouble after, running into the fields and pretending to borrow a pony for a ride home." While living in Quincy, MA, Pat visited with his Aunt Bridgie regularly, including during her time at Marion Manor nursing home. He talked of her lovingly, still today. Mary Meade, Pat's wife, once said to me that "Bridgie's life was a prayer."

Bridget Meade Quealy died on December 28, 1986 at the age of ninety-eight. I had not seen my grandmother in many years, perhaps since 1967 or so, a period of nearly twenty years. I wrote earlier of this abrupt end to any visits or relationship with my extended family. The reason or reasons for it remain, for me, unknown. Memories of her, though, are clear and distinct. Bridget Meade left her mark with me. I feel sure that it is my memories of her Irish accent and of her Irish expressions and of her Irish stories that has long urged me to uncover things unanswered and unknown about our Irish family history.

My grandfather, John Quealy, died many years before Bridget, on March 4, 1957. He was 66 years old. I was not yet four years old and have no real memory of him.

CHAPTER FIVE

The Rising, the Rebels and the start of a Republic

"What in the world's history was ever more romantic than the gesture of a few young men who challenged England when she had a million of men in arms, and died, and won by dying?"
—Stephen Gwyn, "Dublin, Old and New"

It had been tried before, of course. A rebellion, a Rising. Each time, met with dismal failure. It was different now, those committed to Irish independence believed. The world was different now, they believed. The opportunity was different now, they believed. Germany had invaded France in August 1914 and Britain immediately declared war against Germany. Britain's trouble might now be Ireland's fortune.

By mid-year, 1915, early plans for a Rising were forming and circulating among Irish Republican leaders and supporters, both in Ireland and in the US.

John Devoy, an Irishman and early member of the Irish Republican Brotherhood (IRB), also known colloquially as Fenians, a reference to mythical Irish warriors, had fled to the US and New York City in 1871 after his release from Millbank Prison in London, where he'd been held for his part in the planning of an Irish uprising. Devoy now served as Head of Clan na Gael, the Irish-American Revolutionary Organization, based in New York City, and was in steady dialogue with the current leaders of the IRB, principally Tom Clarke, Joe Plunkett and Patrick Pearse. While that group, one afternoon, was discussing the recent death of Jeremiah O'Donovan Rossa, a much-admired old Fenian, a grand idea was struck.

O'Donovan Rossa had, like Devoy, been an early member of the secret and banned Irish Republican Brotherhood. He'd spent many years in British prisons after his capture in 1860, including periods of solitary confinement with arms shackled behind his back, mostly due to his role with an Irish Nationalist newspaper, "The Irish People". Released in 1871 and exiled from his homeland, he fled to New York City, together with John Devoy, and lived out the remaining years of his life there.

O'Donovan Rossa, especially brave and defiant while tortured by his British jailers, was celebrated across Ireland as an authentic and true hero of the Irish struggle for independence. His courage inspired all those who believed in such a cause.

Tom Clarke, in the course of the discussion with Devoy and others about O'Donovan Rossa's death, suggested that the body be brought home to Ireland for a grand funeral and burial and that the occasion be used to excite a nationalist pride among the people of Ireland. A dramatic gesture was needed, said Clarke, to demonstrate the extent of popular support for a new Rising. Surely, the spectacle of mourners by the thousands from across Ireland, grieving the death of a dedicated leader of the IRB, would suit the purpose. Pearse should deliver the oration at the grave.

It was Sunday, August 1, 1915 when the body of Jeremiah O'Donovan Rossa was removed to Glasnevin Cemetery in Dublin and it was there that Pearse rose to speak his tribute to Rossa's memory and to extoll his reputation as a beloved leader.

"...We pledge to Ireland our love, and we pledge to English rule in Ireland our hate" spoke Pearse to a crowd of better than 14,000 who had gathered in respect of such a man as Jeremiah O'Donovan Rossa. "This is a place of peace, sacred to the dead, where men should speak with all charity and with all restraint; but I hold it a Christian thing, as O'Donovan Rossa held it, to hate evil, to hate untruth, to hate oppression, and hating them, to strive to overthrow them. Our foes are strong, and wise, and wary; but strong and wise and wary as they are, they cannot undo the miracles of God, Who ripens in the hearts of young men the seeds sown by the young men of a former generation. And the seeds sown by the young men of '65 and '67 are coming to their miraculous ripening today. Rulers and defenders of realm had need to be wary if they would guard against such processes. Life springs from death, and from the graves of patriot men and women spring live nations. The defenders of this realm have worked well in secret and in the open. They think that they have pacified Ireland. They think that they have purchased half of us and intimidated the other half. They think that they have foreseen everything. They think that they have provided against everything; but the fools, the fools, the fools! They have left us our Fenian dead, and while Ireland holds these graves, Ireland unfree shall never be at peace."

The crowd was hushed and tearful as Pearse ended his eloquent and brilliant eulogy. But it was, as Tom Clarke had hoped it would be, more than a eulogy, more than a tribute to a fallen hero, more than a remembrance of a soldier of the fight. It was a call to the nation, a call to awaken the yearning to finally throw off the rule of a foreign government, to reach yet again for an elusive independence, to take for themselves that which was truly their own and not to be undone. Things had now been set in motion which could not be held back, inexorable, sure as the tides of the Irish Sea. Indeed, those seeds sown in the hearts of young men would ripen in 1916.

The Easter Rising of 1916 was, in the aspirations of its leaders and architects, meant to ignite a final rebellion against British colonial rule and produce, at long last, a free and independent Irish republic. Rebel leaders seized the General Post Office (GPO), a key Government building in the center of Dublin, and several other locations nearby, on April 24, Easter Monday. Patrick Pearse, Commander General of the IRA forces, standing in front of the GPO, read aloud a proclamation of Irish independence, boldly declaring the "...right of the people of Ireland to the ownership of Ireland." British occupation and oppression must no longer be suffered as the new Irish patriots decreed that "...Ireland...summons her children to her flag and strikes for freedom." A green flag emblazoned with the words "Irish Republic" was quickly raised atop the building.

IRA forces, as planned, had also established armed garrisons at other locations around the city, including Jacobs Factory, Sackville Street, The Four Courts, St. Stephen's Green and more, hoping to slow the ability of the British to mobilize additional troops, which would surely be summoned to subdue the Rising and to remove IRA Volunteers from those fortified positions which they now held.

Six days of bitter armed battle followed. The British response to the rebels and to their cause was overwhelming and brought devastation to the whole of the center city of Dublin. Shops, businesses and homes were destroyed and huge fires burned throughout the downtown. The British military had unleashed upon the new Irish patriots and upon the citizens of Dublin the ruin which only a relentless use of artillery, incendiaries, machine guns and even gunboats on the River Liffey could yield. Some 260 civilians were killed in those days, caught inescapably in the blaze of bullets, shelling and fire which had now come to the center of Dublin.

Friday night began still another resounding British artillery assault on the streets around and nearby the GPO. Many of the old city's grand buildings in the area were destroyed or ablaze, brought to rubble by the terrible onslaught. Dublin's Fire Brigades were unable to respond to the growing fires due to the intensity of the fighting between IRA forces and British forces.

Near Moore Street, the Flag Pub had caught fire early on Saturday morning, April 29th, and its owner, Robert Dillon, together with his wife, Ellen, and daughter, May, fled the burning building, all the while holding and waving a white flag to indicate their civilian status. British machine gunners fired without regard, killing Robert in the street. Ellen and May huddled around his body, desperately hoping to survive the attack. Minutes passed before the two, traumatized and grief-stricken, made their way to safety.

Patrick Pearse witnessed the horror, having himself narrowly escaped the inferno which consumed his original command post at the GPO and now occupying a floor atop Coogan's Grocery Shop at the corner of Henry and Moore Streets. Not wishing to abandon his revolt against British rule nor his aim of achieving a free and independent Ireland, it was, nevertheless, clear to him that the unapologetic and callous murder of citizens was intolerable. He knew then that to press on with the Rising would surely result in further bloodshed and death for more innocent people in Dublin, a tragedy he could not abide. He would surrender.

It was on Saturday, April 29th, 1916 at 3:45pm that Patrick Pearse, Commander General of the IRA Volunteers, surrendered to General John Maxwell, recently appointed as General Officer Commanding British Forces in Ireland. Maxwell would, in the coming days, pronounce a cruel and merciless sentence on Pearse and on his fellow leaders of the Rising.

The people of Dublin and of much of the surrounding countryside were resentful—not supportive—of the rebels. The cause of Irish freedom was seen as foolhardy and doomed to failure, sure to bring about only British anger and vengeance. The immediate days following did little to assuage that feeling, as curfews were imposed, food shortages plagued the city and its residents found destruction and ruin all around them where once calm and steady commerce had been enjoyed.

The Second City of the Realm lay smoldering, all due, many felt, to the misguided and reckless adventures of a few Republican rebels. Sentiment ran high against the leaders of the Rising by the time of Patrick Pearse's surrender to British Military authorities and they were jeered and rebuked by crowds as they were marched by British soldiers through the streets of Dublin en route to the Richmond Barracks. "Death to the bloody Shinners" (a reference to members of the new political party advocating for Irish independence, Sinn Fein) was shouted at the rebels all along the route. The people of Dublin generally disowned them and denounced their ill-fated rebellion. The Rising had failed utterly. The British, though, soon made a fateful miscalculation.

A Court Martial was convened under the direction of British General Blackadder and the leaders of the Rising—of the rebellion—were quickly tried and convicted. Courageously, none elected to enter a plea of "not guilty", believing any such claim to be nonsensical. Each was proud of his role—his guilt—in striking against the tyranny of a colonial oppressor and unwilling to disavow it.

After calling each of the seven signatories to the Proclamation of the Republic before the Court and hearing only brief statements, the officers of the Court, without even retiring for consideration, announced the unanimous verdict of "guilty".

General Blackadder called General John Maxwell with news of the verdict and told him "we await your decision, sir". "Shoot 'em" Maxwell replied immediately, not troubling to give the matter a moment's thought.

And so they were shot, one by one, each facing a firing squad in Kilmainham Gaol between May 3 and May 12, 1916.

The stories of their devotion to the cause of a free Ireland and of their singular courage in pursuing it are remarkable both for their sadness and for their inspiration. Some of the stories, in particular, add greatly to the collective story of all of Ireland in its long and difficult and often tragic history. The story of Joseph Mary Plunkett is surely among those.

Joe Plunkett, along with all other of his comrades whose names were affixed to the Proclamation of the Republic of Ireland, was transferred to Kilmainham Gaol immediately after his Court Martial, there to await execution by firing squad. He requested—and was granted—permission to marry his beloved Grace Gifford before his death sentence would be carried out. The two were married in a small chapel in Kilmainham Gaol late on the evening of May 3, 1916, seven hours before Joseph Mary Plunkett faced a firing squad in the early morning of May 4. He was 28 years old. Grace never remarried.

Grace's sister, Muriel, had herself been widowed one day earlier, on May 3, 1916, when her own husband, Thomas Mac Donough, had also been executed by firing squad for his role in the Rising.

Brothers Patrick and Willie Pearse were executed on May 3 and May 4, respectively, 1916. Patrick Pearse was the author of the Proclamation of the Republic. Just days earlier, he had fearlessly told the officers of the Court Martial "...you cannot conquer Ireland. You cannot extinguish the Irish passion for freedom. If our deed has not been sufficient to win freedom, then our children will win it by a better deed."

In a final poignant moment—mournful, courageous, defiant—before his execution and the execution of brother, Willie, Patrick Pearse wrote a poem he titled "The Mother". It expressed his vision of the suffering and of the grief that his own mother must now endure, losing her two sons at the hands of British firing squads:

> *I do not grudge them: Lord, I do not grudge*
> *My two strong sons that I have seen go out*
> *To break their strength and die, they and a few,*
> *In bloody protest for a glorious thing,*
> *They shall be spoken of among their people,*
> *The generations shall remember them,*
> *And call them blessed;*
> *But I will speak their names to my own heart*
> *In the long nights;*
> *The little names that were familiar once*
> *Round my dead hearth.*
> *Lord, thou art hard on mothers:*
> *We suffer in their coming and their going;*
> *And tho I grudge them not, I weary, weary*
> *Of the long sorrow—and yet I have my joy:*
> *My sons were faithful and they fought.*

The public mood, which had, at first, been angry and resentful at the rebels turned toward sympathy and admiration, even guilt at having failed to support their brave exploits, as the executions continued, day after day, through the first weeks of May 1916. The news of the death of one rebel leader, followed by news of the next and the next and the next produced a powerful reaction against the British and the beginnings of a new and more committed zeal toward ending the curse of British rule. The people of Ireland could not long hold the belief that breaking a law which was not a law made in Ireland or acting against a monarch or a government not their own was any crime worthy of execution. Republicanism—by that fateful British miscalculation—was vividly reawakened.

Great Britain, in 1916, remained embroiled in the horrors of World War One and the conflict was taking a heavy toll on the Empire. The situation in Ireland was of secondary importance and, accordingly, the most recent of the several Home Rule bills (i.e., establishment of an Irish Parliament in Dublin, though still to be a subordinate part of the United Kingdom) proposed for Ireland was deferred. John Redmond, the single-most ardent and influential leader of the Home Rule platform, now actively encouraged fellow Irishmen to support the British war effort in what proved to be a vain hope that a grateful British nation would surely grant Home Rule at war's end. How many more times would trust in the British be misplaced?

The results of Redmond's exhortations were mixed. Many Irish men did enlist in the British Army, perhaps as many as 200,00 by most estimates. The prospect of receiving an enlistment bounty, together with regular pay and food, found appeal among many of the enlistees, some 40% of whom were poor and unemployed. Many others in Ireland, though, saw England's war as Ireland's opportunity and believed that a time would soon arrive when Ireland might, at very long last, win its freedom from the iron fist of the British.

Indeed, the stirrings of Irish Republicanism did continue to grow across all the counties of Ireland. British mis-judgements and arrogance only aided this new thinking among the people. Conscription (a draft) of Irish young men was proposed in April 1918 and was met with huge resistance and never implemented; the Great War and its terrible impact had grown unpopular; deferral of Home Rule legislation had bred resentment and the still-lingering anger at the British response to the Rising remained a dangerous flash point.

It was in this tumult that the British General Election of 1918 was held in December and it was all of those factors which led to the dramatic gains of the Sinn Fein party, taking 73 of the total 105 seats allotted for Irish representation in Parliament. Sinn Fein had expressly and publicly declared its intent to establish an independent Republic of Ireland and support for that position was now, without doubt, the majority view.

The party, founded only in 1905, had never before stood in a General Election yet now enjoyed a landslide victory. It is also particularly noteworthy that the General Election of 1918 was the first election in which women over the age of thirty were allowed to vote. Much change was afoot and much would follow.

The newly-elected Sinn Fein representatives, in a resounding act of defiance, unanimously refused to be seated in Parliament and declared Irish independence in January 1919. The outlaw Irish Government, Dail Eireann, was quickly formed, finally realizing the full definition of the victorious political party's name: Sinn Fein, "ourselves alone".

The new Dail Eireann declared that Irish independence was now irreversibly established "...by withdrawing the Irish representation from the British Parliament, and by denying the right and opposing the will of the British government or any foreign government to legislate for Ireland, by making use of any and every means available to render impotent the power of England to hold Ireland in subjection by military force or otherwise."

The flame was lit and the fire now burned across all of Ireland.

CHAPTER SIX

Three Brothers, Bravery and the British

A story of Joe, Peter and Jim Meade and brave service in the Mid Clare Brigade

"My poor people, they have made a Calvary of your little square, but what was meant for a massacre has become a consecration."
—*Bishop of Killaloe, addressing residents of Miltown Malbay after the shootings at Canada Cross, April 14, 1920*

"This little town has suffered more than any other little town in Ireland in the past twelve months. If suffering be the price of national freedom, then Miltown has paid more than its share…"
—*Rev. Hannon, parish priest of St. Joseph's Church, Miltown Malbay, addressing congregation at Sunday Mass after IRA ambush on British Forces and the death of Black & Tan officer Stanley Moore on March 31, 1921. Notably, Peter and James Meade served as scouts for the IRA Mid Clare Brigade during this action.*

The Irish War of Independence came harshly to Miltown Malbay. Though Bridget was now far and safely removed from its dangers, residents of the small town in the West of Clare where she had lived until only a few years prior would soon suffer its scourge. Bridget's family—the Meade family—would come to know particular hardship and sorrow.

The 1918 Elections in which Sinn Fein won a large majority of seats in Parliament proved, of course, to be the seminal moment in the struggle to gain independence from Britain and it was in the Meade household that many local election planning meetings had taken place.

"It is in this, my house, that all the Republicans meet every night to plan out everything… everything was planned for every election, even the County election and they appoint one for every district to go around the day before to tell the old people to be ready when they come for them in the morning. Joe that does as far as Killernan and all the way round to Miltown until 9 O'clock at night and then they go to Ennis with the boxes fearing anything would happen and stay overnight in Ennis…" recalled Ellen Meade some years later, also writing that "…he (Joe) worked hard at the elections bringing voters to the booths every time and never asked a cent." If Republicanism had taken root in County Clare, it flourished in Miltown Malbay.

It was, though, increasingly dangerous to engage in such activities, considered by the British as treasonous and surely likely to invite very intimidating surveillance and ruthless discipline. "I could be writing forever about all we have gone through here during the Troubles" reads one letter of Ellen Meade "...so often raided as they had to pass here and always watched us."

Great Britain emerged from the long and ugly struggle of World War One as the preeminent military power on earth, still able to proclaim both that "Britannia rules the waves" and that the "sun never sets on the British empire." The Armistice had been agreed to in November of 1918 and Britain and its allies had won a decisive and fulsome victory. The British could now attend, uninterrupted, to the "Irish problem".

Beginning in early 1919, Miltown Malbay was designated by the British as a "Military Area" and the Royal Irish Constabulary (RIC) in the town had been reinforced by British Army regulars. "The district was subject to all the objectionable restrictions associated with military rule. Fairs and meetings were banned, movements of persons into and outside the area was allowed only on the production of a permit from the sergeants of the RIC, barricades were erected on the roads at different points in the area at which sentries were posted who questioned and searched pedestrians and passengers in carts and motor cars."

The British, at war's end, were both able and willing to train all the resources of a modern highly-equipped military, including land and naval forces, on the task of finally subjugating these troublesome Irish. Regular British Army troops and the infamous Black & Tans (named for the uniform of Khaki slacks and a black tunic) arrived in Ireland, battle-tested from fighting on the continent and ready to take up arms again in assisting the Royal Irish Constabulary in the aim of destroying Irish hopes for independence. Barracks across Ireland were now filled with experienced and well-armed and well-trained soldiers, all arrayed against a citizen army of volunteers.

The Irish Volunteers, now to be known as the Irish Republican Army, was not an army at all. The IRA had yet no functioning government or state able to fund them or to equip them or to train them, but neither could any state nor any government nor any hostile force deter them from a rigid determination to find themselves freed from centuries-long suffering and oppression. It was necessary to rely on sympathetic and supportive Irish

Americans for money and for arms, smuggled into Ireland at great risk. Germany, too, had earlier assisted the nascent IRA in providing rifles and ammunition, hoping to weaken the English as an adversary.

While British forces could rely upon the use of every implement of modern warfare—tanks, artillery, gunboats, armored carriers, machine guns, mortars, incendiaries—the IRA relied exclusively on guerilla warfare tactics, raiding barracks for weapons, trains and depots for ammunition, hindering British troop movements by blocking roadways with debris or by digging ditches and ambushing British troops along rural country roads where the terrain and routes of escape were familiar.

Tensions were high across the whole of Ireland and surely so in Miltown Malbay. Expressions of disdain and contempt for British occupiers were common and rarely disguised. The ill-will displayed towards Crown Forces was returned aplenty to the citizens of this little town in County Clare. A deadly confrontation would soon result.

British authorities, in January of 1920, arrested a large number of prominent Republicans and remanded them to Mountjoy Prison. The prisoners, led by Tom Hunter, Frank Gallagher and Peadar Clancy, decided on a hunger strike as a means of protesting their unjust incarceration. The hunger strike and the harsh treatment of the prisoners gained wide attention and scorn. Political pressure arising from wholesale public anger eventually persuaded the British to release the prisoners. The news was celebrated across the country. Unfortunately so in Miltown Malbay.

Residents in town, learning the news of the end of the hunger strike and of the release of the Irish political prisoners from Mountjoy Prison, gathered spontaneously on the evening of April 14, 1920 in a location at the town's center called Canada Cross. Canada Cross is the intersection of Ballard Road, Main Street, Ennistymon Road and Church Street. The place had taken its name "in honor of a raid by 'the Bold Fenian Men' who crossed the border from America into Canada in 1866 to raid for arms from the British."

The crowd was jubilant, the celebration festive, the emotion heartfelt and, as the evening progressed, a large tar barrel was set in the center of the intersection and set alight while the crowd sang patriotic songs. One witness described the crowd: "they were...good-humoured and were singing songs... orderly and in no way truculent towards anybody."

Sometime near 10:45pm, fearing that any large gathering in Miltown Malbay could result in public disorder or disruption, forces of the Royal Irish Constabulary arrived on the scene and quickly surrounded the crowd. A Sergeant called on the townspeople to disperse and soldiers immediately opened fire. Opened fire on a crowd of unarmed civilians. Opened fire on a crowd of men, women and children. Opened fire on a crowd of Irish persons, no less, in 1920, citizens of the United Kingdom than would be a crowd gathered in the center of London.

Three Miltown Malbay men—Patrick Hennessy, age 30 and father of two, John O'Laughlin, age 25 and Timothy O'Leary, age 38, father of ten children—were struck by the soldier's bullets and died in the street. Scores of others were wounded and injured, including two schoolchildren, Thomas Reidy and Nonie Donnelon, both under 15 years of age. It is remarkable to consider that, as the Meade family was so connected to the movement for Irish independence and that young Meade brothers were then serving in the Mid Clare Brigade, it is very likely that Meades were among the celebrants—were among those terrified citizens—on that tragic and frightening evening in April of 1920.

While an inquest was organized by British authorities to investigate the shootings at Canada Cross, predictably no punitive actions were taken against any participating members of the Royal Irish Constabulary. And worse, that terrible incident would not be a singular outburst of British anger at the townspeople of Miltown Malbay, but only foreshadowed greater and more deadly trouble to come.

Volunteers, despite the obvious and present threat posed by more and more aggressive military action taken against the people of Ireland, continued to meet in remote locations and to train and to drill and to strategize in preparation for armed battle with their occupiers. We know that Meade brothers—Joe, Peter and Jim—were engaged with the IRA's Mid Clare Brigade at this time and among those readying for the coming conflict, all the while in danger of detection and arrest by the RIC.

Even before the Canada Cross massacre, fatal encounters with British forces had become more common in the West of County Clare in 1920. Just a few months earlier, in fact, Martin Devitt, a Vice Commander of the Mid Clare Brigade, had been shot and killed during a failed raid undertaken to secure rifles from a British barracks.

As Devitt and three other men of the Mid Clare Brigade initiated the raid at Crowe's Bridge in Inagh, several unwitting civilians had crossed into the line of fire. Devitt ceased firing and rose from a crouched position, only to be shot through the head. He died instantly. A comrade, Ignatius O'Neill, was gravely wounded and taken to Miltown Malbay for treatment and recovery. He would later play an instrumental role as Commander of the Rineen ambush, carried out largely as revenge against the British for the killing of Martin Devitt and of the shootings and murders at Canada Cross. A letter from Ignatius O'Neill is contained in the Military Pension files relating to his familiarity with young Peter Meade's IRA service and with the events leading to his death.

The Rineen Ambush is a milestone in the Irish War of Independence and, at the time of its occurrence on September 22, 1920, it was, according to historian Padraig Og O Ruairc, "...the largest and most successful military action against the Royal Irish Constabulary and the Black & Tans that had then taken place in the Irish War of Independence."

The site of the ambush was Drummin Hill, Rineen, a very short distance—perhaps three miles or less—from the town center of Miltown Malbay. The site was chosen for both its height above sea level and because there was a large curve in the road which would cause approaching vehicles to slow speed of travel. Attackers would have a key strategic advantage.

It had earlier been learned by IRA Volunteers, through intelligence reporting, that a British lorry traveled along the road between Ennistymon and Miltown Malbay on every Wednesday morning. The lorry passed by Drummin Hill, Rineen, en route. IRA Battalion leaders, including Ignatius O'Neill, determined that Rineen would be the ideal site for an action and ambush against Crown Forces. The death of Martin Devitt and those murdered at Canada Cross could then be avenged and a large cache of weapons and ammunition could no doubt be seized. The date was set for September 22, 1920.

Early on that morning, armed Volunteers were placed in position to await the arrival of the lorry and a number of scouts were dispersed throughout the surrounding countryside in order to alert the attacking party on any approach of British soldiers. Shortly before noon, a signal of "Ford lorry traveling" was relayed among several of the scouts and, by the time it reached O'Neill, was misinterpreted as "four lorries traveling". He immediately ordered his men to hold fire, fearing that the British traveling

...hey had planned or trained to ...rry passed and the mistake was

... Clune, a Volunteer from Inagh, to ...port on the lorry's position. Clune ...lock that afternoon and reported that the ... barracks in Miltown Malbay and had been ...ion. It might soon, he thought, be returning

...rect, and within a few minutes time, the sound of ...arly heard coming along the road. A signal shot was ...ained their guns on the lorry and on the soldiers ...ish troops were killed instantly and a sixth hurriedly jum... ...icle, running fast toward the coast. He was pursued and shot to dea... ... 300 yards or so. Several British rifles, one revolver and over 3,000 rounds of ammunition were collected by the IRA Volunteers at the scene. Some of the Volunteers were still searching for more ammunition when scouts urgently alerted them that several lorries loaded with armed British troops were coming directly toward them now from the direction of Ennistymon.

The British did quickly, by coincidence and not by design, come upon the IRA ambush party and engaged them in fierce gunfire, even setting up a machine gun near the top of Drummin Hill. Fighting and efforts by the IRA men to escape continued for some three hours, as slow progress was made across fields, through streams, along stone fences and stacks of hay. Much of the captured ammunition was expended in the retreat and two Volunteers—O'Neill and Micklo Curtin—were injured. Both were taken into Miltown Malbay where they were treated by Dr. Michael Hillery. The men recovered fully within a few weeks.

A combination of circumstances and fortune had enabled O'Neill and members of his brigade to make it to the safety of Lahinch and Miltown Malbay: first, the British were entirely surprised to come upon the ambush and therefore unprepared for the combat; additionally, the IRA men were now well-armed and were also far better acquainted with the land, terrain and small, hidden farm roads that were scattered across this countryside in the West of Clare. The escape succeeded but terror would soon visit the town with a frightening vengeance.

It was early in the evening of September 22, 1920, just hours after the Rineen Ambush, that British reprisals got underway. Ernie O'Malley recalls in his book "Raids and Rallies" that "an old man, Keane, had been carting hay to a rick with his horse and cart. He was found to be a good target for soldiers who had followed the lorries and they shot him."

Ernie O'Malley's account continues: "In the nighttime, an RIC raiding party went to old Dan Lehane's house at Cragg near Lahinch...they questioned him about his IRA sons and they threatened him with revolvers when he refused to answer. They explained in tortuous detail what they would do to his boys when they found them...they brought him out to the strand with his wife and, as he stood close to her, they fired a surplus of lead into him. Early the next morning, they burned his house." Dan's young son, Patrick Lehane, was burned to death in the attic.

The violence and horror in Miltown Malbay began near 11:30pm on that Wednesday night. Residents were awakened and startled by rifle shots and by uniformed men shouting in the streets and breaking shop windows and doors. The home of Mr. P.H. O'Neill, father of Ignatius O'Neill, was the first of many to be targeted that night and it was set ablaze and left to burn completely.

Next, multiple shops in the center of town were vandalized and set on fire, British troops making good and widespread use of "petrol" and incendiary devices. The fires were intense and none of the buildings lasted more than thirty minutes before crumbling to the ground.

Looting and destruction continued throughout that long, dreadful night in Miltown Malbay and another eight homes were totally destroyed before soldiers left the town—now very much in ruin—around 5:00am. It was said that no glass could be found in the town except for splinters.

Condemnation of British brutality followed in the international press and even in Great Britain, as some English citizens found the actions taken against an unarmed civilian population, against women and children, old and young, to be an outrage. British Government officials, however, shared little of that sentiment.

The British Labour Party introduced a resolution in the House of Commons condemning the reprisals. It was defeated by a vote of 346 to 79. Hamar Greenwood, the Chief Secretary for Ireland, even defended the actions of

Crown Forces, self-righteously protesting that "...houses destroyed were those of notorious Sinn Feiners." A dubious justification. Independence for Ireland, it was made clear again, would be hard-won. Britannia indeed "...ruled the waves" and, it seems, "...waived the rules."

A poem of Jim Meade's contains a verse which is haunting, especially as we know that he and brothers Joe and Peter were among the local Volunteers in the Mid Clare Brigade at this time in 1920:

"Revenge was sought and revenge was wrought that day in dark Rineen
For Hennessy, O'Leary, O'Laughlin* and Mairtin**
Our gallant sons, they manned their guns, they rushed to freedom's fray
But their high desires brought midnight fires to old Miltown Malbay"

Hennessy, O'Leary and O'Laughlin were residents shot and killed by British forces at Canada Cross in Miltown Malbay in April 1920

**"Mairtin" is the Irish language name for "Martin", a reference to Martin Devitt, a Mid Clare Brigade Volunteer shot and killed by British soldiers in February 1920 at Crowe's Bridge, Inagh*

Events in the small town of Miltown Malbay during this period of Ireland's War of Independence would surely be cast as war crimes today. The cruelty of indiscriminate firing at homes and businesses; of burning houses, shops, farms and crops; of random killings of civilians, no matter the age; modern weapons of war—grenades, machine guns, petrol and incendiaries—all employed against a civilian population appear not very unlike scenes from Ukraine in 2023.

And so it unsettles me to know that the Meade family was there, heard the gunfire, saw the blazes, knew the dead, felt the fear. Ellen Meade, in fact, wrote sadly of son, Michael, in a letter a few years later. "We blamed Michael's insanity on all the frights we had here...they dragged him out of bed one morning to ask about a dance for the prisoners at the house next door (NOTE: dances were often held at family homes as a means of raising funds for imprisoned friends) they burned everything in that house and ran right into ours and said they'd burn ours too..." she wrote. Perhaps Michael's "insanity" might be better known today as Post Traumatic Stress Syndrome, a condition easily recognized on the sad and frightened faces of young victims of war and violence all across our globe a full century later: Syria, Ukraine, Afghanistan and more.

I did talk directly with Pat Meade during my June 2022 visit to Miltown Malbay about Michael and about his grandmother's letter and reference to "Michael's insanity". "Michael was the most kind man you could ever meet... he always was great to me and my brothers and, even more than my father, taught us how to hunt fox and rabbits...he was kind and gentle" Pat told me.

Interestingly, Michael Meade worked on the family farm with his brother, Joe, for many more years, remained involved in the lives of brothers, sisters, nieces and nephews, lived in Miltown Malbay throughout his entire lifetime and died in October of 1993 at the age of ninety-four. Pat dismissed the idea of Michael as "insane" and told me "you can cross that one off your list." Perhaps Ellen Meade's 1920's-era description of Michael Meade as "insane" may be attributable to a shallow understanding of the effects of trauma on a twenty-one-year old boy rather than to a reliable diagnosis.

The Mid Clare Brigade remained active in the Miltown Malbay area even after the sacking and the burning of the town in September 1920. Throughout the War of Independence, the Brigade carried out a number of raids against various targets such as barracks housing troops of the Royal Irish Constabulary, rail stations, British Government tax offices and Post offices and an ambush at Wilson's Pub on March 31, 1921, this time directed against Black & Tans in the town. Military records and witness statements of IRA members at the time make clear that two young Meade brothers–Jim, now a few weeks shy of his sixteenth birthday, and Peter, eighteen years old–served as two of several scouts for this particular IRA action. Pat Kirby, a historian in Ireland's National Defense Forces, told me during our meeting in Inagh in June 2022 that the IRA often recruited and relied upon young teenaged boys to serve as scouts and despatch runners, believing that youth made them less likely to arouse British suspicions.

Peter was a scout in an Active Service Unit (ASU) of the Mid Clare Brigade, 4th Battalion. He often "ran despatches" to various persons and units of the IRA and was detained and questioned and physically harassed on multiple occasions by British armed forces.

It was mid-March of 1921 when Brigade leaders met to plan the attack to take place at Wilson's Pub on March 31 in Miltown Malbay. The date was chosen because IRA intelligence knew that officers of the Black & Tan regiments would be paid their stipends on that day. It was also known that those same officers, flush with cash on paydays, would spend much time on those evenings drinking in local pubs, Wilson's sure to be among them.

John Jones, the Brigade's 4th Battalion Intelligence Officer, planned the logistics of the attack. "I met the attacking party on the Ballard Road just outside the town about nine o'clock pm" Jones wrote years later. The Battalion Volunteers took up positions in the ruins of a home which had been destroyed in the reprisals after the Rineen Ambush and which was located directly across from Wilson's Pub, where "the Tans" were congregated.

Around "half nine" (9:30pm), two Black & Tan officers appeared in the doorway of the pub, engaged in conversation with Mr. Wilson. The attacking party, in order to be sure not to accidentally harm Mr. Wilson, was instructed to wait until the "Tans" departed. A short few minutes passed, and both officers, Constables Moore and Hersey, strode away. Gunfire rose from the attackers and both Black & Tan officers fell immediately. Constable Moore was killed and Constable Hersey wounded.

Captain Edward Lynch, 4th Battalion, Mid Clare Brigade, writing to the Military Pensions Board in support of a Pension for Peter Meade (to be awarded posthumously) stated that:

"Deceased (Peter Meade) was a member of the Fianna Eireann (Irish National Boy Scouts)...he acted as a Scout for the Volunteers who attacked the enemy at Miltown Malbay on 31st March, 1921. The attack was followed by official reprisals in the village on 6th April 1921 by the enemy. The deceased was ordered, after this date, with two other Scouts, to visit the village and keep the local Volunteers in touch with the movements of 'the Tans', whilst he was engaged in this work the enemy became aware of his activities and started paying him attention...".

The Fianna Eireann was established to promote "...the independence of Ireland through the training of the youth of Ireland, mentally and physically, and to achieve this object by teaching scouting and military exercises, Irish History, and the Irish language". It was a rebellious and dangerous pursuit, expressly so in Miltown Malbay, the town having been declared a "Military Area".

The Meade household was regularly under watch by the British and was ransacked in a search for weapons more than once as Peter's activities—and those of brothers Joe and James—brought high suspicion. "My son Joe joined the IRA since it first started...and had arms but was never caught," Ellen Meade once recalled, "although our house was searched three times by the Black & Tans". British hostility remained an ever-present threat. "...My poor husband got a punch of a rifle one morning when he hadn't the door opened quick enough..." Ellen Meade later wrote.

Peter, despite his youth, once thought to shield him from British mistrust, came very directly and tragically into danger. It was especially his role as a lookout and messenger in the ambush of March 31, 1921 that drew the attention of British troops. He "...was attacked by British military on two occasions, and owing to their watching him he was afraid to return to his home..." according to statements of Dr. Michael Hillery.

While on the run, routinely sleeping outdoors in the hills around Miltown Malbay, Peter contracted "acute pneumonia" and died on May 12, 1921 attended by Dr. Michael Hillery, his mother (Ellen Meade) and sister, Katie Meade. He was eighteen years old.

It was determined that Peter's death was a direct result of hiding and sleeping in fields and trenches over the course of several cold and wet days and evenings in that early Spring of 1921, made necessary due to the watchful and menacing eye of British troops who were then carefully monitoring his activities.

Only two months had passed since the death of Peters' older brother, Pvt. Patrick Joseph Meade. The two wars which had claimed the lives of Meade brothers in such quick succession were, of course, very different. But the anguish and the grief were very much the same.

Peter was posthumously awarded a Military Pension in 1938 after the Military Pension Board reviewed and verified his IRA service, scores of corroborating witness testimonies, examination of the Mid Clare Brigade Activity logs, statements from Brigade Volunteers and Officers and certification of Dr. Hillery. The Board concluded, as noted earlier, that "...conditions endured by him, while on the run from British forces, led to his illness and death." Ellen Meade, beneficiary, was paid the Military Pension.

Many years later, after validating information provided in a Medal application, Jim Meade, youngest of the Meade brothers, was also recognized for his courageous service in the IRA's Mid Clare Brigade, with the Military Pensions Service Collection recording "...service certified and duly-awarded medal issued...".

No funeral for young Peter was ever held, as martial law prevailed across all of County Clare in 1921 and the fear of British troops in the nearby area firing on any large gathering in Miltown Malbay—as they had done before—was real and prevalent.

A Truce was signed on July 9, 1921—less than sixty days after young Peter Meade's death. The sorrow made only greater.

Patrick Pearse had warned the British during his Court Martial in 1916 that Irish freedom would one day be won "...by a better deed" than that undertaken by him and by his fellow leaders of the Rising. British General Maxwell, to the contrary, declared that "I am going to do something that you Irish will never forget. I am going to ensure that there will be no treason whispered, even whispered, in Ireland for another hundred years."

Pearse, the rebellious Irishman, was sure of his country's ambitions for freedom and of the will of its citizens to achieve it. Maxwell, the British General, was equally sure that he could produce a fear among the Irish people sufficient to subvert any quest for—any whisper of—independence for at least one hundred years.

A treaty establishing the Irish Free State was signed in December of 1921, a mere five years after each man—Pearse and Maxwell—had made their bold predictions. Pearse, it seems, was the better prognosticator.

CHAPTER SEVEN

A Love for Ireland, at Home and Away

"How my soul did grieve when I had to leave your radiant rock-bound shore"
—James (Uncle Jim) Meade

Ellen Meade, we remember, had once written about her husband Peter that "...his country was always his trouble and every one of his children are the same at home and away...".

Peter Meade's children were, indeed, "...the same at home and away..." in their love for Ireland and in their commitment to advancing the fortunes of that beloved homeland.

Some expressions of that deep affection and commitment were both kind and sentimental:

> *Bridget caring for a brother wounded in the Great War; returning, for a time, to home in 1913 and forever remaining in contact with family there and with brothers, sisters, nieces and nephews; singing an Irish lullaby to grandchildren and helping to purchase the original Meade headstone in Ballard Cemetery in memory of her father;*

Some were found in active engagement and efforts to promote prosperity in Ireland:

> *John and Jim's leadership in multiple Irish civic and cultural organizations; Jim Meade's Boston Globe obituary notes that he was, in Boston, an "...Irish cultural leader;'*

Some were rooted in gratitude and sacrifice for a brother, John, who'd been steadfast in his dedication to the family as a young boy in Ireland:

> *Katie's selfless caring for John's young children in a time of great need and tragedy; it would be, for her, a life-long devotion;*

And some were deeply courageous and heroic:

> *Jim, Joe and Peter's valiant service in the IRA's Mid Clare Brigade, always at great personal risk against a merciless and well-armed occupying enemy.*

Jim Meade, at one time, served as president of the Central Council of Irish County Clubs in Boston and addressed that group on St. Patrick's Day, March 17th, 1944:

"One of the irritations that bother all men sincerely interested in Ireland's cause is the partition of the island...the partition of Ireland is nothing more, nor less, than disunion. And Ireland will not take her proper place among the nations until this disunion is dissolved and she stands triumphant in the loving gaze of her sons and daughters scattered throughout the world, united as a nation from her topmost northern boundary to her most southerly shore."

A love for Ireland, at home and away.

CHAPTER EIGHT

Going Back

"My heart is quite calm now. I will go back."
—James Joyce

And so this history of ruthless landlords, of tenant farmers, of boycotts and rebels and republicans, of the Black & Tans, of courage, resistance, reprisals, of emigration, of distant lands and places unwelcoming, of tragedies and sorrows, of sacrifice, of devotion to this place from whence the first beat of our very hearts would one day come, of grief, of endurance and of renewal is our history today. It beckons us toward a homeland that has always been alive in us and, indeed, it calms the heart when we go back.

Jim Meade expressed many thoughts and sentiments throughout his life in original poetry. He wrote poems for his children upon graduation from high school; about the memory of his father; about the valor of his friend, neighbor and comrade in the Mid Clare Brigade, Patrick Kerin; about the beauty he found surrounding him as a child in Miltown Malbay; about the courage of those who would defy the power of the landlords; about the suffering felt by the people of that small West Clare town.

Jim emigrated to the United States in 1927 at the age of 22 and joined his brother John and his sister Katie then living in Boston. Ireland, though, had taken its hold on him and he could never fully leave it behind. "...With tear-dimmed eyes and heartbreak sighs, I left Miltown Malbay" he once wrote wistfully.

He returned often to Miltown Malbay and it is clear that deep affection for Ireland stirred in him on each such occasion. "Since we left the good old USA, bound for our native shore, our ship draws nearer to the land we all adore" he wrote on June 14, 1932 from the deck of the USS President Harding as the grand liner steamed headlong for Ireland.

And it is here today, June 9th, 2022, almost precisely ninety years later, on the West Coast of County Clare, embraced by the Irish countryside, soothed by the whisper of an Irish breeze, calmed by the rhythms of an Irish sea, spellbound by the colors of an Irish sky, that I am moved to remember them, to learn of them, to speak of them, to write of them.

The time and efforts I've spent and journeys I've made in pushing to uncover and to learn about all the travails that the Meade family experienced as a poor tenant farming family in a turbulent, violent and pivotal time in Ireland has enriched me. The inexplicable longing to understand this deep Irishness in me, awakened so long ago, is now made more vivid. "My heart is quite calm now. I will go back".

POSTSCRIPT

❖ My meetings and discussions with Pat Meade while visiting Miltown Malbay in June 2022 were especially rewarding and interesting, yielding stories of a young "Bridgie" (Bridget Meade) and of her lasting interest in family and in events in Miltown Malbay; of Katie's remarkable and unselfish life and of her humor; of Michael's devotion to his nephews and of his kind and gentle nature; of scorn once held for the landlords in the time of Peter and Ellen Meade; of admiration for the courage of the citizens of Miltown Malbay in resisting British rule and authority and of the uneasy divisions which arose after the signing of the Treaty with Britain in December 1921, even among immediate family members. Joe Meade, Pat's father, was anti-treaty (Fianna Fail party); Pat, in his adulthood, came to associate with the Fine Gael party, with its history dating to the "pro-Treaty" viewpoint championed originally by Michael Collins; Pat recounted that, on the subject of the Treaty, which remains controversial even today, "I couldn't speak of it in my own house...I never could understand it" (i.e., opposition to the Treaty and Michael Collins); I've met with Pat in Ireland a few times over the years and remain in touch with him by telephone conversations from time to time;

❖ Pat once co-owned a pub in South Boston with Jake Rooney, "The Casino"; Pat had lived in Quincy, MA for nearly 35 years before returning to full-time residency in Miltown Malbay in 2000;

❖ Pat and Fr. John Meade had a long and very friendly relationship with Monsignor Kickham, who married me and Joanie;

❖ Pat's children:
  • Joe lives in Marshfield and is a nurse at Boston Medical Center;
  • Maura lives in Nova Scotia;
  • Marguerite lives in Quincy and works for Stop & Shop;

❖ Still living in Miltown Malbay (as of August 2022):
- Pat Meade
- Michael Meade
- Gerard Meade
- Chrissy Curtin, Meade cousin. Mary (Curtin) Meade married Joe Meade (Bridget's brother) and is mother of Pat, Michael, Gerard, Peter, Fr. John and Mary
- Joanie Madden (Meade cousin, daughter of Helen Meade Madden) is founder and leader of a celebrated Irish musical group, "Cherish the Ladies", and is widely considered to be the greatest Irish flute player of her generation; Joanie's grandfather, Jim Meade, and my grandmother Bridget Meade, were first cousins, children of brothers Michael and Peter Meade;

❖ Pat Meade put me in touch with Joanie Madden after my June 2022 meeting with him and Joanie and I attended a "Cherish the Ladies" concert in, remarkably, Lowell, MA in July of 2022; we met with Joanie Madden briefly back-stage after the concert, having arranged the meeting with her via email;

❖ Pat Meade remembers uncle Brendan Quealy visiting Miltown Malbay while serving in the US Army and stationed overseas in the 1950's;

❖ Pat Meade knew Larry Quealy very well during all the years that Larry worked in the administrations of Mayors Kevin White and Ray Flynn;

❖ Uncle Jim was instrumental in the original effort to unionize the staff of prison guards at the Charles Street Jail and, just as with other civic and cultural organizations with which he was involved, Jim Meade served in leadership positions, becoming president of Local 1134 of the State, County and Municipal Employees Union; his son, Jimmy Meade, is recently retired after serving for many years as Superintendent of Library Buildings in the Boston Public Library system. Jimmy and Theresa (Terry) live in Dorchester. They have four children and three grandchildren. We're now in touch regularly.

❖ Peter (Pat's brother) and Mary Meade live in Westwood, MA and return often to Miltown Malbay. As with Jimmy and Terry and Pat, Peter and I are in touch periodically.

Joanie and me at Boston College, 2013, with then-Prime Minister of Ireland Enda Kenny; we've enjoyed BC-Irish connections for many years which were helpful in researching this story

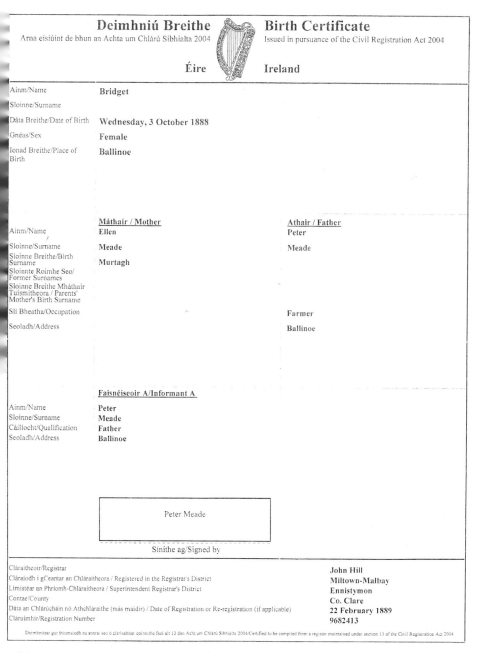

Deimhniú Breithe   **Birth Certificate**

Arna eisiúint de bhun an Achta um Chlárú Sibhialta 2004   Issued in pursuance of the Civil Registration Act 2004

Éire   Ireland

Ainm/Name	Bridget
Sloinne/Surname	
Dáta Breithe/Date of Birth	Wednesday, 3 October 1888
Gnéas/Sex	Female
Ionad Breithe/Place of Birth	Ballinoe

	Máthair / Mother	Athair / Father
Ainm/Name	Ellen	Peter
Sloinne/Surname	Meade	Meade
Sloinne Breithe/Birth Surname	Murtagh	
Sloinnte Roimhe Seo/ Former Surnames		
Sloinne Breithe Mháthair Tuismitheora / Parents' Mother's Birth Surname		
Slí Bheatha/Occupation		Farmer
Seoladh/Address		Ballinoe

Faisnéiseoir A/Informant A

Ainm/Name	Peter
Sloinne/Surname	Meade
Cáilíocht/Qualification	Father
Seoladh/Address	Ballinoe

Peter Meade

------- Sínithe ag/Signed by -------

Cláraitheoir/Registrar   John Hill
Cláraíodh i gCeantar an Chláraitheora / Registered in the Registrar's District   Miltown-Malbay
Limistéar an Phríomh-Chláraitheora / Superintendent Registrar's District   Ennistymon
Contae/County   Co. Clare
Dáta an Chlárúcháin nó Athchláraithe (más maidir) / Date of Registration or Re-registration (if applicable)   22 February 1889
Cláruimhir/Registration Number   9682413

Deimhnítear gur thiomsíodh na sonraí seo ó clárleabhar coinnithe faoi alt 13 den Acht um Chlárú Sibhialta 2004/Certified to be compiled from a register maintained under section 13 of the Civil Registration Act 2004

Bridget Meade's Irish Birth Certificate

69

Town Clerk's Office, Brookline, Massachusetts

CERTIFIED COPY OF RECORD OF MARRIAGE

PATRICK JOSEPH WARD
Town Clerk

No. **165**	Date of Marriage	**June 4, 1919**	Place of Marriage	**Brookline**

	Groom		Bride
Name	**John Quealy**	Name	**Bridgie Mary Meade**
Surname after Marriage	————	Surname after Marriage	————
Age Date of Birth	**28**	Age Date of Birth	**27**
Number of Marriage	**First**	Number of Marriage	**First**
Widowed or Divorced	————	Widowed or Divorced	————
Residence	**Brookline, Massachusetts**	Residence	**Brookline, Massachusetts**
Occupation	**Janitor**	Occupation	**Maid**
Birthplace, City/Town and State	**Ireland**	Birthplace, City/Town and State	**Ireland**
Name of Father	**Michael Quealy**	Name of Father	**Peter Meade**
Name of Mother (Maiden)	**Bridget Reidy**	Name of Mother (Maiden)	**Ellen Murtagh**

Name, Residence, and Official Station of Person who Solemnized Marriage
Rev Garrett J. London, 158 Pleasant Street, Brookline, Massachusetts, Priest

Date of Record   **June 5, 1919**

I hereby depose and say, that I hold the office of Town Clerk of the Town of Brookline, in the County of Norfolk and the Commonwealth of Massachusetts; that the Records of Marriages in said Town are in my custody, and that the above is a true extract from the Records of Marriage in said Town, as Certified by me.

WITNESS my hand and the SEAL of the said TOWN of BROOKLINE,

on this **28th** Day of **July** A.D. 20 **14**

Attest: _____
Town of Brookline, Massachusetts

Bridget Meade and John Quealy Marriage Certificate

70

Grandmother Bridget holding me and includes my sisters, Suzie and Ginny and our cousins, Noreen and Sheila Quealy

Standing, left to right: Brendan, Priscilla, Mary Lou, Larry, Phife, Johnny, Tommy, Mary, Vinnie, Anne; seated, left to right: Theresa, Bridget, Helen

Miltown Malbay more than one hundred years ago

Miltown Malbay today

Maguire's Forge in Miltown Malbay still operates today; Sarsfield Maguire was one of the famous "three brave blacksmiths"

A mural depicting the "three brave blacksmiths" is prominent in the center of town, at the corner of Ballard Road and Main Street in Miltown Malbay, June 2022

St. Joseph's Church, long a centerpiece of the town

Plaque at the entrance to St. Joseph's Church in Miltown Malbay commemorating all those who died in the Parish in various tragic circumstances through the years, a stark reminder of the many sufferings endured by residents of the town

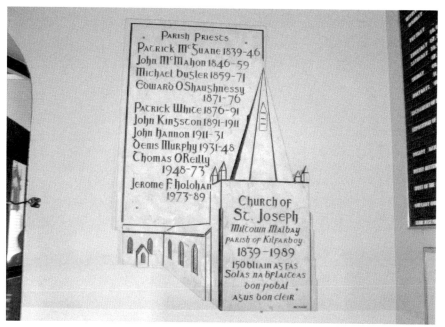

Plaque at entry foyer to St. Joseph's Church listing priests who served the Parish over the years; note the listing of Fr. Patrick White (1876-1891), who is featured in the story of Peter and Ellen Meade and married the couple in 1885; also Fr. Hannon (1911-1931) who addressed parishioners after the IRA ambush of Black & Tans at Wilson's Pub in Miltown on March 31, 1921

Peter and Ellen Meade and the 10-acre farm; they operated the farm first as tenants (1885) and, beginning in 1916, as owners; all of the Meade children were born here; the original house still stands (and is occupied though not by Meade family); note shed (background, right) which is the place we've visited many times

General Valuation of Rateable Property in Ireland.

ACTS 15 & 16 VIC., CAP. 63, AND 17 VIC., CAP. 8.

UNION OF ENNISTIMON.

VALUATION OF THE SEVERAL TENEMENTS

COMPRISED IN THE ABOVE-NAMED UNION

SITUATE IN THE

COUNTY OF CLARE.

RICHARD GRIFFITH,

Commissioner of Valuation.

ʀED AT THE GENERAL VALUATION OFFICE, No. 2, FITZWILLIAM-PLACE, DUBLIN,

this 12th day of September, 1855.

Treasurer of the County of Clare, and
To the Clerk of the Board of Guardians of the
Ennistimon Union.

ices of intention to Appeal are to be addressed to the Clerk of the Board of Guardians of the Ennistimon Union.

DUBLIN:

PRINTED BY ALEX. THOM AND SONS, 87, ABBEY-STREET,

FOR HER MAJESTY'S STATIONERY OFFICE.

1855.

PARISH OF KILFARBOY.

No. and Letters of Reference to Map.	Names. Townlands and Occupiers.	Immediate Lessors.	Description of Tenement.	Area. A. R. P.	Rateable Annual Valuation. Land. £ s. d.	Buildings. £ s. d.	Total Annual Valuation of Rateable Property. £ s. d.
	BALLYNEW—*continued.*						
7 a	Bridget Sullivan,	Francis Goold Morony,	House and land,	9 3 1	3 15 0	0 5 0	4 0 0
	James White,				0 5 0	—	0 5 0
·8	John Frawley,	Same,	Land,	1 2 20	0 5 0	—	0 5 0
	John Lenehan,				0 5 0	—	0 5 0
9 a		Same,		0 2 7	3 15 0	0 5 0	4 0 0
10 A	Patrick Sullivan,	Same,	House, office, & land,	3 1 17	1 5 0	—	
— B				1 0 7	0 10 0	—	2 5 0
— C				1 0 7	0 10 0	—	
11 a	John Murtough,	Same,	House, office, and land,	10 3 0	3 10 0	0 10 0	4 0 0
— b	Board of Nat. Education,	Same,	Nat. school-ho., & yard,	—	—	1 0 0	1 0 0
12 a	Johanna Kenny,	Same,	House and land,	0 3 12	3 15 0	0 5 0	4 0 0
13 A	Bartle Kenny,	Same,	Land,	5 3 16	1 15 0	—	2 5 0
— B				1 3 8	0 10 0	—	
— A a b	Daniel Downes,	Same,	House and garden, (See lot 16.)	0 0 39	0 2 0	0 6 0	0 8 0
14 a				23 0 5	7 10 0	1 10 0	9 0 0
15 A	Anthony Sullivan,	Same,	House, office, & land,	2 2 1	1 0 0	—	
— B				1 0 7	0 8 0	—	1 18 0
— C				1 0 37	0 10 0	—	
16 A				11 1 27	3 0 0	—	
— B	Daniel Downes,	Same,	Land,	1 3 0	0 15 0	—	5 5 0
— C				3 2 24	1 10 0	—	
17 A				6 3 10	2 10 0	—	
— B	John M'Caw,	Same,	Land,	0 3 35	0 8 0	—	3 8 0
— C				1 0 16	0 10 0	—	
18 a	James Sullivan,	Same,	House, office, and land,	10 0 34	6 15 0	0 5 0	7 0 0
			Total,	307 3 27	99 4 0	9 1 0	108 5 0
			EXEMPTIONS:				
11 b	Board of Nat. Education,	Francis Goold Morony,	Nat. school-ho., & yard,	—	—	1 0 0	1 0 0
			Total, exclusive of Exemptions,	307 3 27	99 4 0	8 1 0	107 5 0
	BALLYVASKIN, NORTH. (Ord. S. 23.)						
1 a	Patrick Dougherty,	Thomas Crowe,	House and land,	15 3 20	2 15 0	0 5 0	3 0 0
2 a	John Crow, jun.,	Michael Crow (John),	House and land,	3 0 13	0 15 0	0 5 0	1 0 0
3 A a	Michael Crow (John),	Thomas Crowe,	House, office, & land,	26 2 21	6 10 0	0 10 0	7 10 0
— B				3 2 15	0 10 0	—	
4 A a				9 1 39	4 0 0	0 5 0	
— D	Patrick Clancy,	Same,	House and land,	5 0 33	0 15 0	—	5 15 0
— C				4 1 35	0 15 0	—	
5 A				65 0 27	14 0 0	—	
— B a	John Mullaghan,	Same,	Herd's ho., offs., & ld.	86 3 34	25 10 0	0 15 0	74 10 0
— C a				75 0 9	34 0 0	0 5 0	
— A a	Honoria Walsh,	John Mullaghan,	House,	—	—	0 5 0	0 5 0
6 A				19 0 1	6 10 0	0 10 0	
— B	Michael Hogan,	Thomas Crowe,	House, office, & land,	1 0 30	0 10 0	—	8 10 0
— C				2 1 10	1 0 0	—	
7 A				2 1 15	0 10 0	—	
— B a	Thomas Frawley,	Same,	House, office, & land,	28 2 4	9 0 0	1 0 0	10 10 0
8 A a				24 3 12	10 0 0	0 5 0	
— B	Patrick Marony,	Same,	Herd's house & land,	11 0 7	2 10 0	—	16 0 0
— C				11 3 25	3 5 0	—	
9 A a	Anne Shea,	Patrick Marony,	House,	—	—	0 5 0	0 5 0
— B a	Michael Crowe (James),	Thomas Crowe,	House, offices, & land,	7 3 35	2 10 0	—	9 10 0
				22 3 35	6 5 0	0 15 0	
10	Patrick Rochford,	Same,	Land,	12 0 3	4 10 0	—	4 10 0
11 a	Thomas Mead,	Same,	House and land,	5 0 25	2 5 0	0 5 0	2 10 0
12 a	John Talty,	Same,	House and land,	14 0 27	4 17 0	0 3 0	5 0 0
13	John Crow, sen.,	Same,	Land,	23 1 35	9 10 0	—	9 10 0
— a	Margaret Marony,	John Crow,	House,	—	—	0 5 0	0 5 0
			Total,	482 1 0	152 12 0	5 18 0	158 10 0

"John Murtagh…Francis Gould Morony as Lessor (landlord)…10 acres, 3 roods… total valuation Four Pounds Sterling"

NO RENT MANIFESTO

'FELLOW-CITIZENS: The hour to try your souls and to redeem your pledges has arrived. The executive of the National Land League, forced to abandon its policy of testing the Land act, feels bound to advise the tenant farmers of Ireland from this day forth to pay no rents under any circumstances to their landlords until Government relinquishes the existing system of terrorism and restores the constitutional rights of the people. Do not be daunted by the removal of your leaders. Do not let yourselves be intimidated by threats of military violence. It is as lawful to refuse to pay rents as it is to receive them. Against the passive resistance of the entire population military power has no weapon. Funds will be poured out unstintedly for the support of all who may endure eviction in the course of the struggle. Our exiled brothers in America may be relied upon to contribute, if necessary, as many millions of money as they have contributed thousands to starve out landlordism and bring English tyranny to its knees. You have only to show that you are not unworthy of their boundless sacrifices. One more crowning struggle for your land, your homes, your lives – a struggle in which you have all the memories of your race, all the hopes of your kindred and all the sacrifices of your imprisoned brothers.

Stand together in face of the brutal, cowardly enemies of your race !

One more struggle in which you have the hope of happy homes and national freedom to inspire you, one more heroic effort to destroy landlordism, and the system which was and is the curse of your race will have disappeared forever. Stand together in face of the brutal, cowardly enemies of your race! Pay no rent under any pretext! Stand passively, firmly, fearlessly by, while the armies of England may be engaged in their hopeless struggle against the spirit which their weapons cannot touch, and the Government, with its bayonets, will learn in a single Winter how powerless are armed forces against the will of a united, determined, and self-reliant nation.[10]

CHARLES S. PARNELL. THOMAS BRENNAN.
A. J. KETTLE. THOMAS SEXTON.
Michael Davitt. PATRICK EAGAN.
John Dillon.[11]

The No-Rent Manifesto, written by Charles Stuart Parnell and other leaders of the Irish National Land League from Kilmainham Gaol, October 1881; it inspired Peter Meade and Fr. Patrick White to organize and protest against local landlords

Death of Prominent Miltown Malbay Man

The death of Mr Peter Meade, of Knockliscraun, Miltown Malbay, which occurred on Saturday, 31st July, was greatly regretted, not only by the friends residing in the neighbouring district, but by his wide circle of friends and relatives residing in many other parts of the county. He was well liked for his generous character. He was a devout Catholic, a patriotic Irishman, and a lover of music and song. As an athlete he met the "peerless" Tom Malone in many competitions. In politics he was a keen follower of Parnell and was connected with all his movements, especially that one which was so beneficient to the people, the "no rent manifesto." His jovial disposition won for him many friends both young and old, all of whom enjoyed his pleasant company. His uprightness and honesty made him an exemplary character. He was the loving father of ten children, six of whom, John, Tom, Anthony, Margaret, Mary and Bridget, are in Boston, U.S.A., where they have made a name for themselves.

The remains were removed to the Parish Church, where they lay overnight. The funeral to the family burial ground at Ballard was of huge proportions, being representative of all classes. Rev Fr. Hughes, C.C., officiated at the graveside.

The chief mourners were Ellen Meade (wife); Joe, Michael, Jim (sons); Katie (daughter); Michael Meade (brother); Mrs Fitzpatrick (sister); Michael Fitzpatrick, Jas. Meade (nephews); Hannah Meade and Mrs Frawley (nieces); Anthony, Michael, Pat, Mary, and Josie Conway; Mary, Thomas, Susan Meade, Miltown; Peter Meade, Mrs Burke, and Katie Meade, Knokliscrane; John, Joe, Mary Meade, Milford, Lizzie Curtin, N.T; Annie Curtin, Ellen McMahon, Frank Moloney, Tom McMahon and Mrs Daly, Miltown; Mrs Barry, Mary, Bridget, Michael Barry, Illane; Ml. O'Connor, John, Mary Anne, Kathleen, Eileen, Lizzie O'Brien, Leeds; John Martin, Bridget and Mrs J. McMahon, Clohaunmore; Mrs McNamara, Mrs White, Mrs O'Donohue, Tim Clancy, Mrs P. White. Glendine; James, Patrick, James Anthony, Martin and Bridget Kerin, Knockliscrane; Mrs Norah White, Cloanemore; Martin McMahon, Martin Moroney, Patrick Marrinan, Mrs Clohessy, Mrs Margaret Clohessy, and Mrs Canny, Ballyvaskin, Ml. Hayes and Mrs Richard White, Miltown; T. G. Burke, Clonlaheen, Mrs O'Loughlin, Shanaway; Tom and Margaret Lynch, Cahereogan, Susan and John Moroney, do; Mrs John O'Brien, Caherogan; John T. Burke, Pat and John Burke, Patk. Sexton and Mike Curtin, Leeds; Peter and Tom Smyth, Fahanlannaghta; Michael Frawley, Mrs Pat Flynn, Miltown; John T. Linneen; Daniel Curtin, Knockbrack; Mrs P. Burke, Breffa; Pat Lynch, and Norah Malone, Kilcornan; Mrs M. Barry, John P. McMahon, Tom P. McMahon, Miltown; Ellen and Thomas Moloney, Moy (cousins.)

Mrs Meade and family wish to express their deep gratitude to all who sympathised with them during their great sorrow.

1926

Peter Meade's Obituary, July 1926; Peter was noted as a "...keen follower of Parnell and was connected with all his movements, especially...the No Rent Manifesto"

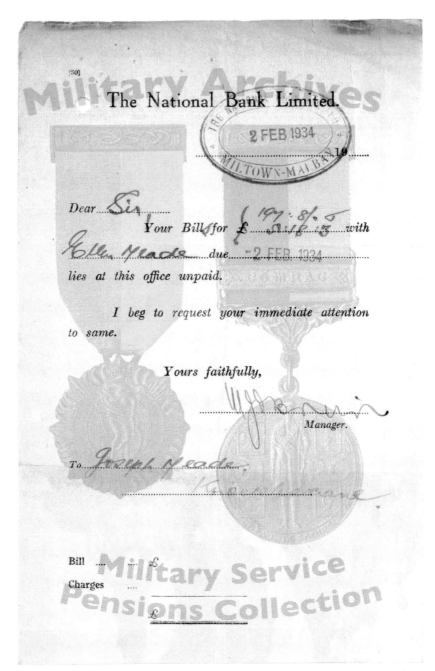

(30)

The National Bank Limited.

2 FEB 1934

MILTOWN-MALBAY 19

Dear Sir

Your Bill for £ 197 8/0 with

Ellen Meade due 2 FEB 1934

lies at this office unpaid.

I beg to request your immediate attention to same.

Yours faithfully,

Manager.

To Joseph Meade

Bill £

Charges

£

A note from the National Bank Limited addressed to Joseph Meade advising of unpaid bill (mortgage) owed by Ellen Meade

Visit to the original Meade farm again, with Pat Meade, June 2022; we first visited here with Pat Meade in 2005; view is from shed looking toward original house; note boundary marker in foreground, right

PROCLAMATION.

WHEREAS by PROCLAMATION given at His Majesty's Castle of Dublin, on the 10th day of December, 1920,

I, JOHN DENTON PINKSTONE, VISCOUNT FRENCH, Lord Lieutenant General and General Governor of Ireland, did proclaim that certain Counties are and until further order shall continue to be under and subject to MARTIAL LAW:

NOW I do hereby proclaim by virtue of all the powers me thereunto enabling that to the Counties named in the said PROCLAMATION of the 10th day of December be added the following counties, namely:

The County of Clare;
The County of Kilkenny;
The County of Waterford;
The County of the City of Waterford;
The County of Wexford;

which Counties are also and until further order shall continue to be under and subject to

MARTIAL LAW

equally and in like manner as are those Counties named by me by PROCLAMATION of the 10th day of December as aforesaid.

Given at His Majesty's Castle of Dublin this 4th day of January, 1921.

FRENCH.

GOD SAVE THE KING.

Printed for His Majesty's Stationery Office by A. THOM & CO., Ltd., Dublin.

British Proclamation of Martial Law, December 10, 1920. Irish independence, the British made clear, would not be easily won.

[Please note that all Copies made on this Page should be certified at foot.]

04398969

Superintendent Registrar's District _Ennistymon_   Registrar's District _Miltown Malbay_   145

19 21   DEATHS Registered in the District of _Miltown Malbay_ in the Union of _Ennistymon_
in the County of _Clare_

No. (1)	Date and Place of Death. (2)	Name and Surname. (3)	Sex. (4)	Condition. (5)	Age last Birthday. (6)	Rank, Profession, or Occupation. (7)	Certified Cause of Death and Duration of Illness. (8)	Signature, Qualification, and Residence of Informant. (9)	When Registered. (10)	Signature of Registrar. (11)
123	Twelfth May 1921 Knockliscrane	Peter Meade	Male	Bachelor	17 Years	Farmer's Son	Acute Rheumotism Three days Heartfailure Certified	Katie Meade Sister of deceased Present at death Knockliscrane	Sixth June 1921	Daniel J. MacBlaney Registrar
124	Tenth June 1921 Miltown Malbay	Jane Anne McCrossan	Female	Widow	80 Years	Old Age Pensioner	Chronic Endocarditis mitral Double Two months Heartfailure	Son West Seventeenth present at death Miltown Malbay	Twentieth June 1921	Daniel J. MacBlaney Registrar
125	Fourteenth April 1921 Rineen	Theresa Curtin	Female	Spinster	Five days Daughter		Weakness from birth Heartfailure uncertified No medical	Catherine Curtin Mother of deceased Present at death	Twentieth June 1921	Daniel J. MacBlaney Registrar

I, _Daniel MacBlaney_ Registrar of Births and Deaths in the District of _Miltown Malbay_ in the Union of _Ennistymon_ in the County of _Clare_ do hereby certify that this is a true copy of the Registrar's Book of Deaths within the said District, and that I have compared it with the Entry of the Death of _Peter Meade_ No. _123_ to the Entry of the Death of _Theresa Curtin_ No. _125_. Witness my hand, this _12th_ day of _July_ 19__.   _Daniel MacBlaney_

I have examined the above, and have compared it with the said Original Registrar's Book, and hereby certify that it is a true Copy. Witness my hand, this _30th_ day of _July_ 19__.   _Richard Griffy_ Superintendent Registrar.

Young Peter Meade's Death Certificate, May 12, 1921; note that his sister, Katie, was "present at death"

ARMY PENSIONS BOARD,
ST. BRICIN'S HOSPITAL,
DUBLIN.

52/APB/525   30th April, 1937.

E. Lynch, Esq.,
   Dept. of Defence,
      Griffith Barracks,
      DUBLIN.

A Chara,

I am directed by the Army Pensions Board to state that they have under consideration a claim under the Army Pensions Act, 1932, from Mrs. Ellen Meade, Knockliscrane, Miltown-Malbay, Co.Clare, in respect of her deceased son, Peter Meade, who died on the 12th May, 1921, the certified cause of death being Acute Pneumonia.

It is stated that the deceased caught cold while on duty in connection with an ambush which took place in or near Miltown-Malbay in April, 1921. The Board will be very much obliged if you will kindly state whether you have any knowledge of the deceased's services in the I.R.A., whether the ambush referred to did take place in April, 1921, and if so, whether the deceased took part as alleged.

I am to request the favour of an early reply and I am to state that any particulars furnished by you will be regarded as strictly confidential.

An addressed envelope, which need not be stamped, is enclosed for your reply.

Mise, le meas,

Rúnaí.

Letter from Army Pension Board to Edward Lynch, who had served in the Mid Clare Brigade, asking for "knowledge of deceased's (Peter Meade) services in the IRA..."

Galway
14th June 1937

Secretary
Military Pensions Board
St Bricin's Hospital

A Chara,

In connection with the claim of Mrs Meade Knockliscrane Miltown Malbay for the loss of her son Peter Meade; the following are the facts of the case which I obtained from reliable sources of both sides.

Deceased was a member of the Fianna Éireann Scouts, and although a good scout in every respect he was of a very nervous disposition. He acted as scout for the Volunteers who attacked the enemy at Miltown Malbay on 31st March 1921. This attack was followed by official reprisals in the village on the 6th April 1921 by the enemy. The deceased was ordered, *after this date*, with two other scouts to visit the village and keep the local Volunteers in touch with the movements of the Tans, whilst he was engaged in this work the enemy became aware of his activities and started paying him attention.

He was working for a farmer at this time and being young & nervous he got the "wind up" to such a pitch that he started sleeping out in outhouses & by ditches, which undermined his health and resulted in his death.

His people are very respectable and have always been connected with the National movement.

Is mise le meas
E Lynch

Reply from Edward Lynch, former Captain in the Mid Clare Brigade, to the Military Pension Board; note that Edward Lynch states that "...the following are the facts of the case..."

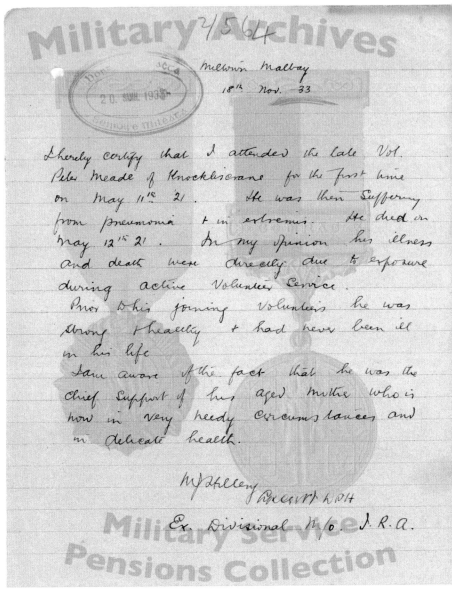

Miltown Malbay
18th Nov. 33

I hereby certify that I attended the late Vol.
Peter Meade of Knockliscrane for the first time
on May 11th 21. He was then suffering
from pneumonia + in extremis. He died on
May 12th 21. In my opinion his illness
and death were directly due to exposure
during active Volunteer service.
Prior to his joining Volunteers he was
strong + healthy + had never been ill
in his life
I am aware of the fact that he was the
Chief support of his aged mother who is
now in very needy circumstances and
in delicate health.

M J Hillery
present LDH
Ex. Divisional M/o. I.R.a.

Letter of Dr. Michael Hillery certifying that he "attended the late Vol. Peter Meade...
suffering from pneumonia in extremis...He died on May 12th '21...directly due to
exposure during active Volunteer service." Note his signature as: "Ex. Divisional M/O
(Medical Officer) I.R.A."

I. The addresses of the following persons whose names are given by you in
your application :—

Name   Address

Dr. M. J. Hillery   *Miltown Malbay*
         Co. Clare

Peace Commissioner

II. Name of Officer Commanding Brigade *Frank Barrett*

Present Address *Ennis Deceased*

III. Name of Officer Commanding Battalion *James Hennessy*

Present Address *Cloneogan Moy Latinok Co, Clare*

IV. Names of your Company Captains or other Officers :—

(1) Name, Rank and Appointment *Anthony Kerin*

Present Address *Knocklis crone Miltown Malbay Co. Clare*

(2) Name, Rank and Appointment *Patrick Kerin*

Present Address *Knocklis crone Miltown Malbay C. Clare*

V. Names and addresses of persons (other than the Officers named above) who
can corroborate the statements in your application as to wounds, injury,
disease (or cause of death) :—

(1) Name *Bryan Gloughlin Glendine*

Present Address .... *Miltown Malbay Co Clare*

(2) Name *Anthony Malone Miltown Malbay*
        Ennis Rd.

Present Address ....

(3) Name *Peter Sexton*

Present Address *Kilcorran Miltown Malbay C. Clare*

Signature *Ellen Meade*

Address *Knocklis crone*
        Miltown Malbay

Date *Sept. 28th 1933*   *C. Clare*

Officers of the Mid Clare Brigade corroborating Peter Meade's service in the IRA
and death resulting from service; note Dr. M.J. Hillery; Brigade Commander
Frank Barrett; Battalion Commander James Hennessy (grandfather of Colin
Hennessy who is listed in my Acknowledgements, as I corresponded and
also met directly in Ireland with Colin. He provided invaluable insights and
information); Company Captain, Anthony Kerin (Anthony Kerin was a neighbor
and long-time friend to the Meade family and served in the Mid Clare Brigade
with Meade brothers. He appears often in the letters of Ellen Meade and in the
Obituary of Peter Meade)

QUERIES:

(1) Between what dates did deceased serve with your Command?

From January 1919 to May 12th 1921

(2) In what capacity did deceased serve?

Despatch rider

(3) In what area was deceased engaged in Military Service?

F Co. 4th Batt. M.C.B.

(4) Did deceased contract any disease during his Military Service as defined? If so, please give the following particulars:—

Contracted bronchitis which developed into pneumonia from which disease deceased died.

(a) Nature of the disease ... ...

Pneumonia

(b) Actual conditions under which deceased performed his Military Service. (A detailed statement of the actual conditions, with dates, under which deceased served, should be given.)

(c) Particulars of any illness from which the deceased suffered during his Military Service. (A detailed statement, with dates should be given.)

Was detailed for special service in connection with the ambush which took place in Miltown Malbay in April 1921 which necessitated deceased to have to spend two nights in the open keeping watch for the local column which took part in the above named ambush

(d) Full particulars of any negligence or misconduct on the part of the deceased which, in your opinion, should be taken into consideration in determining whether the disease was attributable to Military Service ... ...

None to my knowledge

(5) Particulars of any other matter in support of the applicant's claim or otherwise, on which you desire to comment. ... ...

Contributed his earnings to his mother, to my own personal knowledge, as he was engaged as a farm labourer

(6) Date of death of deceased ...

12 May 1921

(7) Have you personal knowledge of the facts of the case as set out by you above, or are your replies based on official reports, or on information otherwise received?

I know the above answer to be correct as deceased was a next door neighbour of mine

I declare above statements to be true to the best of my knowledge, information and belief.

Signature *Anthony Kerin*

Organisation and Rank *O.C. Fianna F Co. 4th Batt. M.C.B.*

Address *Knocklicrane Miltown Malbay Co. Clare*

Date *Sept 28. 1933.*

Official Statement of Anthony Kerin, O/C (Officer Commanding) Fianna (scouts), F Co., 4th Batt. M.C.B. (Mid Clare Brigade) to the Military Pensions Board verifying circumstances of Peter Meade's death and IRA service

QUERIES:

(1) Between what dates did deceased serve with your Command? — *Between 1919 and 1921*

(2) In what capacity did deceased serve? — *As a Boy Scout.*

(3) In what area was deceased engaged in Military Service? — *Mid Clare Area.*

(4) Did deceased contract any disease during his Military Service as defined? If so, please give the following particulars:— — *Yes.*

  (a) Nature of the disease ... ... — *Pneumonia.*

  (b) Actual conditions under which deceased performed his Military Service. (A detailed statement of the actual conditions, with dates, under which deceased served, should be given.) — *Deceased always performed his military duties in a very efficient manner. He contracted a bad cold on the night of the Milltown Reprisals as he was running dispatches for his Coy Capt.*

  (c) Particulars of any illness from which the deceased suffered during his Military Service. (A detailed statement, with dates should be given.) — *Deceased was always strong and healthy prior to this*

  (d) Full particulars of any negligence or misconduct on the part of the deceased which, in your opinion, should be taken into consideration in determining whether the disease was attributable to Military Service ... ... — *There was no negligence or misconduct in the case of deceased. He was a well disciplined obedient Boy Scout. He often had to run dispatches in most inclement weather.*

(5) Particulars of any other matter in support of the applicant's claim or otherwise, on which you desire to comment. ... ... — *Applicant is now a widow in poor circumstances. She always shared any spare cash that she had with those that were interned or on the run for which she never looked for or received any compensation*

(6) Date of death of deceased ... — *(approx) 1921 12th May*

(7) Have you personal knowledge of the facts of the case as set out by you above, or are your replies based on official reports, or on information otherwise received? — *I have personal knowledge of the facts of above case.*

I declare above statements to be true to the best of my knowledge, information and belief.

Signature *James Hennessy*
Organisation and Rank *I.R.A Ex O.C 4th Battn. Mid Clare Bgde.*
Address *Clooneyogan. Lahinch. Co Clare.*

Date *Oct 6th 33.*

Official Statement of James Hennessy, I.R.A Ex O/C (Officer Commanding) 4th Battn. Mid Clare Bgde. (Brigade) to the Military Pensions Board verifying circumstances of Peter Meade's death and IRA service

20. IUL 1934

Knochliscrane 18, July, 1934.

Dear Sir

I Anthony Kerin of Knochliscrane being Company Capt of, F, Company, Oglaigh Na h-Eireann 4th Batt, Mid Clare, B, Y, D. can certify that the statement of Mrs Ellen Meade.

Knochliscrane Miltown Malbay Co Clare, is perfectly true that the deceased Peter Meade of Knochliscrane, Miltown Malbay, Co Clare, was an active member of, F, Company, Oglaigh, Na Eireann, and served as despatch rider for the A, S, U, 4th Batt. M, C, B, from January 1919, to May the 12th 1921.

Signed Anthony Kerin
Co Capt, F boy, 4th Batt
M, C, B

Letter from Anthony Kerin of F Company Mid Clare Brigade further attesting to his knowledge of Peter Meade's service in the IRA (Oglaigh Na hEireann) as a " ...despatch rider for the A.S.U. (Active Service Unit), 4th Batt. M.C.B." (Mid Clare Brigade)

Ref. No. 52/APB/525. A.P. 21.

Army Pensions Acts, 1923 to 1932.

CLAIM FOR DEPENDANTS' ALLOWANCE OR GRATUITY.

Applicant's Name *Mrs. Ellen Meade,*

Address *Knocklisscane,*

Miltown - Malbay, Co. Clare

Name of Deceased *Peter Meade.*

*Force to which Deceased belonged *Oglaigh na h - Eireann (I.R.A)*

Date of Death of Deceased *12th May 1921*

Relationship of Applicant to Deceased *Mother.*

PARTICULARS OF DECEASED'S CHILDREN IN RESPECT OF WHOM ALLOWANCE IS CLAIMED.

Name	Date of Birth
do.	do.
do.	do.
do.	do.
do.	do.
do.	do.

Particulars of Payments made from Army Funds to Applicant since death of Deceased.

---

*Oglaigh na h-Eireann (I.R.A.), Irish Volunteers, Irish Citizen Army, 1916, Fianna Eireann, Hibernian Rifles, Cumann na mBan, Defence Forces.

Official Application by Ellen Meade for Dependent's Allowance or Gratuity arising from Peter Meade's service in Oglaigh Na hEireann (IRA)

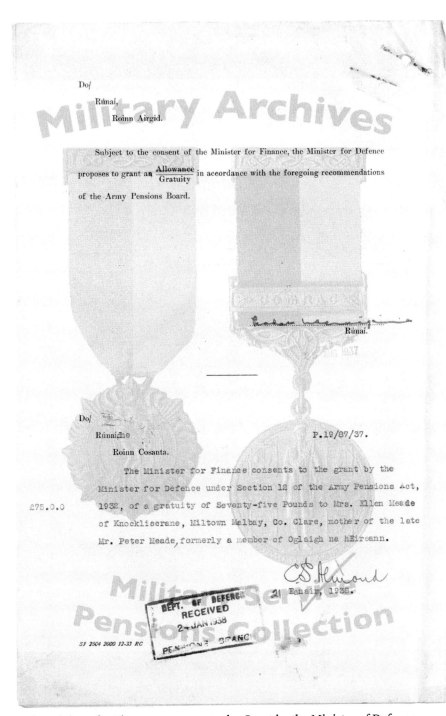

Do/

Rúnaí,

Roinn Airgid.

Subject to the consent of the Minister for Finance, the Minister for Defence proposes to grant an ~~Allowance~~ / Gratuity in accordance with the foregoing recommendations of the Army Pensions Board.

Rúnaí.

Do/

Rúnaidhe

Roinn Cosanta.

P.19/87/37.

£75.0.0

The Minister for Finance consents to the grant by the Minister for Defence under Section 12 of the Army Pensions Act, 1932, of a gratuity of Seventy-five Pounds to Mrs. Ellen Meade of Knockliscrane, Miltown Malbay, Co. Clare, mother of the late Mr. Peter Meade, formerly a member of Oglaigh na hEireann.

21 Eanair, 1938.

SF 2504 2000 12-33 RC

"The Minister for Finance consents to the Grant by the Minister of Defence... to Mrs. Ellen Meade...mother of the late Mr. Peter Meade, formerly a member of Oglaigh Na hEireann"

No. D.P.3052.
Y/347.

ARMY PENSIONS ACTS, 1923 to 1932.

a. s. Rúnaidhe,

A.P. 25.

27/1/38

AWARD CERTIFICATE.

Any further Communications
on this subject should be
addressed to—
and the above number quoted.

AN ROINN COSANTA,
(DEPARTMENT OF DEFENCE),

BRAINNSE PINSEAN AN AIRM,
(ARMY PENSIONS BRANCH),

GEATA NA PAIRCE,
(PARKGATE),

BAILE ATHA CLIATH.
(DUBLIN).

January, 1938.

I am directed to inform you that your claim for an allowance or gratuity in respect of the death of your **son** has been considered by the Army Pensions Board, and to state that the Minister for Defence has approved of the Board's recommendation of an Award in your case, as shewn below.

a.s. RUNAI.

*To Mrs. Ellen Meade,

Knockliscrane, Miltown Malbay,

Co. Clare.

Issued 27/1/38

MD.

Rate per		From	To	Remarks
£ s. d.	£ s. d.			
75.-.-.				
(Seventy-five pounds)				
(Gratuity)				

N.B.—This Certificate is no security whatever for debt. It should be carefully preserved, as it will be of the greatest assistance to you when completing the Payment Draft which will be sent to you.

*In the event of the death of the person to whom this Form is addressed, the person who notifies the death to the local Registrar of Deaths should deliver this Form and any other Pension papers held by deceased, to him, and will receive from him the sum of one shilling for so doing.

SP 3429 1000 2-36 RC 2/32770

Army Pensions Acts, 1923-1932, Award certificate indicating to "Mrs. Ellen Meade" that "...the Minister for Defence has approved of the Board's recommendation of an award in your case..."

#OnThisDay **12** #May **1921** - Peter Meade DP3052, F Coy, 4 Btn, Mid Clare Bde, IRA, died at home at Knockliscrane, Miltown Malbay of acute pneumonia contracted while on active service. Noted that he slept out in the open for two nights after an ambush of British forces in April **1921**.

"tweet" from Military Pensions Service of May 12, 2021, the 100th anniversary of young Peter Meade's death resulting from his IRA service

 **James Meade:**

File Reference	MD47755
Name	James Meade
Address detail	
Street	Knockliscrane, MiltownMalbay
County	Clare
Country	Ireland
Date of birth	1905-04-19
Notes	File relates to successful Service (1917-1921) Medal application. Service certified and duly awarded medal issued 2 September 1971.
Data Protection Note	Open
Organisation	Fianna ÉireannIrish Republican Army
Rank	Unknown
Commanding Officer(s)	Seamus Hennessy; Daniel McMahon; Anthony Malin
Company	F Company
Unit	4 Battalion
Brigade	Mid Clare Brigade
Medal awarded	Service (1917-1921) Medal

IRA service certified and a medal "duly awarded" on September 2, 1971
to James Meade, youngest of the Meade children

Dr Michael Hillery

There were many "unsung" heroes during the War of Independence namely, those behind the scenes who did Trojan work and without whom the campaign for freedom could not have succeeded. These "behind the scenes" patriots included: the members of Fianna Eireann, and Cumann Na mBan, those who provided safe houses and looked after the welfare of the men "on the run", and of course the members of the Medical profession who, often at enormous risk to themselves tended to those who were wounded. Dr. Curran, Ennistymon, Dr Peterson, Lisdoonvarna, Dr Garrahy, Ennistymon, Dr. Hayes, Kilmaley, Dr. Mc Donagh, Quin, Dr McClancy, Ennistymon, Dr. O'Dwyer, Ennistymon. Dr Keane Ennistymon and Dr. McGovern, Lahinch, are names that immediately come to mind of those who provided sterling service.

A name consistently mentioned as providing medical assistance was that of **Dr. Michael Hillery of Milltown Malbay.** During the War of Independence he was called on many times to to attend to sick and wounded I.R.A. men, sometimes under the most difficult and dangerous travelling conditions. On occasions many of these missions were to isolated areas and had to be made on foot. Following the attack at Crowes Bridge, Inagh, (in which Commandant Martin Devitt was killed) Ignatius O'Neill was critically wounded, Dr Hillery was called on to render medical aid. After a diagnosis of the wound, he expressed grave concern at his condition and said that it was of the utmost importance to have him removed immediately to a nursing home, where proper medical aid could be provided. At the time few people were aware that the private nursing home to which he was removed was none other than Dr Hillery's own residence, located within sixty yards of the headquarters of the Black and Tans in Milltown Malbay. After the Rineen ambush he was again called on to give medical aid when Michael Curtin and his former patient Ignatius O'Neill had become victims of enemy bullets. These are but a few of the many deeds he performed.

This "unsung hero" in the Fight for Independence served his country and fellowman without notoriety or decoration and never expected any. He was a true patriot and a credit to the Medical profession. Prior to his retirement in 1957 Dr. Hillery was M.O.H. for the Miltown Malbay district and Corroner for West Clare. He also practised in the Meath Hospital, and as a lecturer at the Royal College of Surgeons, Dublin.

Publication: Connacht Tribune; Date: Oct 26, 1957; Section: None; Page: 19

Death Of Doctor Who Aided The Wounded 'On The Run'

NEWS of the death of Dr. Michael Hillery, which took place at his residence, Spanish Point, on Wednesday last, evoked regret throughout the county.

His services to the sick and wounded during the War of Independence will long be remembered. After the famous Rineen ambush Dr. Hillery brought to his own home in Miltown Malbay Ignatius O'Neill and cared for his wounds

Full military honours were rendered at the funeral to Ballard Cemetery. Members of the

ENNISTYMON AND NORTH CLARE

Old I.R.A. carried the remains from Spanish Point to Miltown Malbay.

He is survived by his son, Dr. P. Hillery, T.D.; Dr. Eleanor Ryan, Dr. B. Hillery and Mr. D. Hillery.

96

John Meade County Clare Association

Thirtieth Annual May Party for Folks of County Clare, Ireland

Committee for the County Clare annual May party. Seated left to right: Mary Flanagan, Elizabeth Lafferty, John Meade, chairman, Babe Shannon. Standing, Mary Kelly, Kathleen Hayes, Rita Kelly and Katherine O'Laughlin.

Elaborate arrangements are now completed for the 30th annual May party and dance of the Knights and Ladies of St. Senan, County Clare Association, which will be held next Thursday evening, May 10, in Cypress Hall, Central square, Cambridge. A well known broadcasting orchestra has been engaged to furnish music.

This event becomes more popular each year and always attracts a large number of natives of the "Banner County," their families and friends, not only from metropolitan Boston, but also from the remotest parts of the State. Last year this affair was the greatest social success in the association's programme for the season and present indications are that the rec-ords of last year will be more than surpassed.

Continual dancing will be enjoyed from 8 o'clock until 12 and the committee in charge of arrangements are leaving nothing undone to ensure an enjoyable evening's entertainment for the large attendance anticipated.

John J. Meade is chairman, Miss Cathleen Lafferty, secretary; Miss Babe Shannon, treasurer, and these are assisted by Michael J. O'Dea, Michael J. Doolin, President John J. O'Loughlin, William J. Hanley, John Flannagan, Thomas Hayes, Michael O'Dee, Elizabeth Lafferty, Cathleen Hayes, Martin J. Kelly, Austin Greene, Cathleen O'Laughlin, Mary Kelly, Mary Flannagan, Rita Kelly and James Meade.

John Meade County Clare Association

MEADE—In Dorchester, Aug. 2, John J., beloved husband of the late Mary F. Meade (nee Shine); residence 25 St. Brendan rd.; father of Sr. Maura, S.N.D., Academy of Notre Dame, Tyngsboro, Sr. Catherine Mary C.S.J., Mt. St. Joseph Academy, Brighton; Peter J. Meade and Mrs. Richard E. Cote of Chelmsford; grandfather of Mary Ellen, Christine and John Cote; brother of Catherine M., Anthony F., Thomas M., James P. Meade and Mrs. John Quealey and Joseph and Michael Meade of County Claire, Ireland. Uncle of Sr. Mary Ernestine C.S.J. St. Raphael Convent, West Medford; Peter J. and Patrick J. Meade of Dorchester. Funeral from the Harold L. O'Neil Funeral Home, 405 Washington st. at Bradlee st., Dorchester on Wednesday, Aug. 5 at 9 a.m. Solemn Requiem High Mass at St. Brendan's Church at 10 o'clock. Relatives and friends respectfully invited. Visiting hours Monday and Tuesday 2-5 and 7-10 p.m. Interment St. Joseph's Cemetery; retired manager Old Harbor Village Housing Project, late member Dorchester Board of Trade, Eire Society, Past president County Claire Assn. and past treasurer Dorchester Real Estate Brokers Assn.

John Meade Obituary

James Meade, 78; founded union, was Boston Irish cultural leader

James P. Meade, 78, of Dorchester, an Irish cultural leader and founder and former president of Local 1134 of the State County and Municipal Employees Union, died Friday in his home after a four-year battle with cancer.

A native of Miltown Malbay, County Clare, Ireland, Mr. Meade was the youngest of 14 children of the late Peter and Ellen Meade. He came to the United States in 1927.

Long active in Irish social and cultural affairs, he also was active in politics and was among the early supporters of John F. Kennedy's political career. Mr. Meade later met Kennedy in Dublin in the summer of 1963. He also was a friend of many Boston politicians.

Mr. Meade earlier had been a guest at the White House of President Dwight D. Eisenhower, when the the so-called Meade Bill was signed in 1955, to allow immigrants who fought in Korea to become naturalized citizens without waiting five years.

Mr. Meade, a family member said, also wrote poetry and songs, some of which were recorded from the 1950s through the 1970s. "His songs were all Irish. But the poetry was of any sort, about important American figures, events with the lyrics rhyming, a family member said.

Mr. Meade was educated in Ireland's national schools.

He was president of Irelands 32, the Clare Club and in 1946 was elected president of the Central Council of Irish County Clubs.

He was a charter member of the Irish Social Club of Boston, and was presiding officer at Irish Inaugural ceremonies. He was the in-

JAMES P. MEADE

stalling officer at most Irish clubs in Greater Boston," his son, Peter of Dorchester said.

He was a retired Suffolk County correction officer and was president of the union 15 years.

Besides his son, he leaves his wife, Mary (Queally) of Doolin, County Clare; four daughters, Eileen Daily of Westbrook, Conn., and Maureen Griffin, Cathleen McDermott and Patricia Meahl, all of Dorchester; another son, James Meade of Dorchester; two sisters, Catherine Meade of Dorchester and Bridget Queaiy of Brookline; a brother, Thomas Meade of Needham, and seven grandchildren.

A funeral Mass will be said today at 11 a.m. in St. Ann's Church, Dorchester. Burial will be in New Calvary Cemetery, Mattapan.

Jim Meade Obituary

Monument at the site of the Rineen Ambush near Miltown Malbay; Jim Meade wrote in a poem "...revenge was sought, revenge was wrought that day in dark Rineen..."; soldier is said to be pointing North to the six partitioned Counties, signaling the quest for a fully united Ireland

Tim, Kerry, Mike on first visit to the original Meade farm, 2005

REGISTRATION CARD | No. 282

Form 1

1 Name in full _John Quealy_ Age, in yrs. 20

2 Home address _7 Floyd St Lowell Mass_

3 Date of birth _Aug 1 89_

4 Are you (1) a natural born citizen, (2) a naturalized citizen, (3) an alien, (4) or have you declared your intention (specify which)? _Declared_

5 Where were you born? _Co Clare_ _Ireland_

6 If not a citizen, of what country are you a citizen or subject?

7 What is your present trade, occupation, or office? _Wool Sorter_ 11

8 By whom employed? _U.S. Worsted Co_ Where employed? _No 6 Chelmsford_

9 Have you a father, mother, wife, child under 12, or a sister or brother under 12, solely dependent on you for support (specify which)? _Father in Ireland_

10 Married or single, which? _Single_ Race (specify which)? _Caucasian_

11 What military service have you had? Rank _____; branch _____; years _____; Nation or State _until Ireland gets national independence_

12 Do you claim exemption from draft (specify grounds) _Whole support of Father_

I affirm that I have verified above answers and that they are true.

ORDER NO. 655 _J Quealy_ (Signature or mark)

John Quealy wrote "none until Ireland gets national independence" when asked to provide his "Nation/State" on the Draft Card Form

20-3-13 **REGISTRAR'S REPORT** A

1 Tall, medium, or short (specify which)? _Tall_ Slender, medium, or stout (which)? _medium_

2 Color of eyes? _Blue_ Color of hair? _Brown_ Bald? _no_

3 Has person lost arm, leg, hand, foot, or both eyes, or is he otherwise disabled (specify)? _no_

I certify that my answers are true, that the person registered has read his own answers, that I have witnessed his signature, and that all of his answers of which I have knowledge are true, except as follows:

N 4

Precinct _3_

City or County _Lowell_

State _Mass_

_____ Mc Greery (Signature of registrar)

June 5/17 (Date of registration)

103

Standing in front of Queally's pub, with owner and cousin Thomas Queally, Miltown Malbay, 2005

Made in the USA
Middletown, DE
27 July 2023